DATE DUE

DEC 0 5 9(

D0378540

MISSION and the PEACE WITNESS

GOLDEN GATE SEMINARY LIBRARY

MISSION and the PEACE WITNESS

The Gospel and Christian Discipleship

Institute of Mennonite Studies
Missionary Studies, No. 7

Robert L. Ramseyer, Editor

HERALD PRESS
Scottdale, Pennsylvania
Kitchener, Ontario
1979

GOLDEN GATE SEMINARY LIBRARY

Library of Congress Cataloging in Publication Data

Main entry under title:
Mission and the peace witness.

  (Missionary studies; no. 7)
  Includes bibliographical references.
  1. Missions—Theory—Addresses, essays,
lectures. 2. Peace (Theology)—Addresses, essays,
lectures. I. Ramseyer, Robert L., 1929-
II. Series.
BV2063.M56   266'.001   79-16738
ISBN 0-8361-1896-0

  Except where otherwise indicated, Scripture quotations are from the
Revised Standard Version of the Bible, copyrighted 1946, 1952, © 1971, 1973.
  Verses marked NIV are from *The New International Version,*
Copyright © 1978 by The New York International Bible Society. Used by
permission of Zondervan Publishing House.
  Verses marked TEV are from *Good News for Modern Man* Copyright © by
American Bible Society, 1966, 1971, 1976. Used by permission.

MISSION AND THE PEACE WITNESS
Copyright © 1979 by Herald Press, Scottdale, Pa. 15683
  Published simultaneously in Canada by Herald Press,
  Kitchener, Ont. N2G 4M5
Library of Congress Catalog Card Number: 79-16738
International Standard Book Number: 0-8361-1896-0
Printed in the United States of America
Design: Alice B. Shetler

15 14 13 12 11 10 9 8 7 6 5 4 3 2 1

CONTENTS

INTRODUCTION

These essays are an attempt by writers from within the peace church tradition to deal with one of the thorniest issues in Christian mission—the issue of just what the Christian gospel is and what it means to become a Christian. This basic issue underlies missionary discussions of "contextualization" and "indigeneity." It is the real issue in the Church Growth Movement's distinction between "discipling" and "perfecting" and in criticisms of applications of "the homogeneous unit principle." It is involved when missionary theologians attempt to distinguish between "gospel" and "ethics."

The writers of these essays are not armchair theoreticians. They bring to this discussion a broad range of personal involvement in mission in radically different settings. In addition they bring a variety of academic disciplines and interests. They are unified, however, in their commitment to faithfulness in Christian mission.

Although no attempt has been made to present a carefully unified point of view throughout these essays, it will be apparent to the reader that the understanding of peace presented here is neither restricted to an inner experience of peace with God nor to a peace which is defined by the absence of war. Peace as these writers use the term is a quality of relationship, a quality which affects all human encounters, a quality which is traced back to the Old Testament term *shalom.*

The basis of these essays is the Bible, both Old and New Testaments. Each writer in his own way attempts to show how the biblical record of God's interacting with human beings guides us in our attempt to be faithful in mission today.

The tone of these essays is one of penitence and of hope, rather than judgment. Taken together their message is that all of us have fallen short in both our understanding and practice of mission and thus robbed the gospel of much of its power to change human lives. They are being published with the hope that they will help all Christians to:

(1) More clearly understand both our message and our mission.

(2) Be able to bring together both in our understanding and in our lives the gospel and that way of living which is Christian discipleship.

(3) Become more faithful missionary servants of Jesus Christ.

Robert L. Ramseyer
1978

1

THE GOSPEL OF PEACE[1]

Marlin E. Miller

Many contemporary evangelical Christians refer to "the gospel" as if the word had a narrowly circumscribed content. "Preaching the gospel" presumably means proclaiming the message of forgiveness from past sin and guilt through the atoning work of Christ on the cross, inviting sinners to repent and accept God's plan of salvation, and extending the promise of eternal life to those who accept Christ as personal Savior. Within the broader Protestant context of evangelical Christianity, "the gospel" also carries the connotation of pure grace, devoid of any ethical demands which might be construed as prerequisites for salvation or as conditions for remaining in a state of peace. Discipleship as the shape of Christian obedience is seen at best as secondary, as a fruit of faith's response to the gospel. It is, however, not understood as integral to the gospel message as such. Major dogmatic definitions have thus attached to the biblical term "gospel," a particular content which provides a capsule statement of the message to be preached. This content is intended also to be a critical safeguard against liberal deviations, for example, against tendencies to seek man's salvation by education, material welfare, or social change rather than by preaching "the gospel."

The New Testament however employs a variety of terms to describe the comprehensiveness of the good news. Jesus Himself proclaimed the gospel of the kingdom. The Apostle Paul speaks about the gospel of God, the gospel of Jesus Christ, the gospel of the glory of Christ, the gospel of salvation, and simply the gospel. Both Peter (Acts 10) and Paul (Ephesians 2, 6) refer to the "gospel of peace." This variety of New Testament terms certainly may not be construed to mean that there are several "gospels" which differ markedly in form and substance. The gospel of God is none other than the gospel of Jesus Christ. The gospel of salvation is the same as the gospel of peace. Even on the most superficial level, this multiplicity of descriptions should caution against too readily limiting our understanding of the gospel to one facet of the New Testament message or against reducing all other dimensions of the good news to one particular aspect. Such reductionist interpretations almost inevitably end up with a truncated gospel, an amputated Christ, and a crippled church. We should rather seek to understand the particular point of reference of each description and its roots and place within the global vision of the good news.

Within the limits of this essay, I will focus on the description of the good news as "the gospel of peace."

This focus is prompted not by an attempt to reduce the good news to a gospel of peace, but by specific shortcomings in broad streams of Protestant and evangelical thought and practice. Sometimes the gospel of peace has simply been omitted from the message as preached. Perhaps more often, "peace" has been reduced to the inner calm of an assuaged conscience, interpreted as "peace with God." Perhaps even more often "peace" has been separated from the gospel and assigned to Christian social ethics. As such it may arise when the topic is discipleship or Christian action in the society at large, but peace is not seen as the immediate focus of the gospel. This theological axiom has also been reinforced in the minds of many Mennonite missionaries as well as congregational members by the institutionalized division of labor between denominational mission boards and the Peace Section of the Mennonite Central Committee. In all of these ways, sometimes more explicitly, other times more implicitly, reconciliation of former enemies and the establishment of peace where prejudice, conflict, and injustice characterize human relations and social structures are not understood as integral to Christ's saving work on the cross.

In comparison to these omissions and interpretative schemes, we may summarize our thesis as follows: Peace as a present social and structural reality as well as an inner tranquility and future promise inherently and explicitly belongs to a biblically adequate understanding of salvation through Jesus the Messiah. It therefore also inherently and explicitly belongs to a mission theology and practice which accepts the New Testament description and proclamation of the good news as normative for Christian mission in our time.

In its major forms, the word "peace" appears over 100 times in the New Testament. The contexts of its usage also demonstrate its significance of the biblical message. God is repeatedly called the God of peace; Jesus is named the Lord of peace; the Holy Spirit is recognized to be the Spirit of peace. After Jerusalem's rejection of the messianic peace offered by Jesus, He gave it instead to His disciples. "Peace" was the characteristic greeting of the early Christians. In using this greeting, they most likely meant to follow Jesus' own practice and to witness to the fulfillment of the messianic peace. When he addressed Cornelius, a Gentile with whom faithful Jews were to have no close association, the Apostle Peter summarized God's message to His people as "the good news of peace through Jesus Christ" (Acts 10:36, NIV). The Apostle Paul encouraged the Christians in Ephesus to "stand firm" with their "feet fitted with the readiness that comes from the gospel of peace" (Ephesians 6:15, NIV). In the same epistle, he summarized the purpose of Jesus' coming and of His death on the cross as the making of peace between Jew and Gentile.

We do well to remember that Jesus and His disciples stood in the tradition of the Old Testament law and prophets (Matthew 5:12). When they spoke about peace and identified the good news of salvation with the gospel of *peace*, they used the term in the Hebraic sense of *shalom*. John Driver has aptly summarized this understanding of peace in *Community and Commitment*, from which we quote extensively:

Shalom is a broad concept, essential to the Hebrew understanding of relationship between people and God. It covers human welfare, health, and well-being in both spiritual and material aspects. It describes a condition of well-being resulting from sound relationships among people and between people and God. According to the prophets, true peace reigned in Israel when justice (or righteousness) prevailed, when the common welfare was assured, when people were treated with equality and respect, when salvation flourished according to the social order determined by God in the covenant which He had established with His people. In fact, the prophet understood that God's covenant with Israel was a "covenant of life and peace" (Malachi 2:5).

On the other hand, when there was greed for unjust gain, when judges could be bought for a price, when there was not equal opportunity for all, when suffering was caused by social and economic oppression, then there was no peace, even though false prophets insisted to the contrary (Jeremiah 6:13-14).

For the Hebrews, peace was not merely the absence of armed conflict. Rather shalom was assured by the prevalence of conditions which contribute to human well-being in all its dimensions. Not mere tranquility of spirit or serenity of mind, peace had to do with harmonious relationships between God and His people. It had to do with social relationships characterized by His people. It had to do with social relationships characterized by justice. Peace resulted when people lived together according to God's intention. Peace, justice, and salvation are synonymous terms for general well-being created by right social relationships.[2]

To be sure, the concept of peace in the New Testament differs in significant ways from this composite image of shalom in the Old Testament. In this respect, the New Testament fulfills and transforms the expectations of the Old. But this fulfillment and transformation does not amount to replacing the Hebraic vision of peace with Greek or Roman views of peace, even though these may be more familiar to those of us shaped by Western culture and accustomed to thinking with its categories. In contrast to a predominantly Greek view, the New Testament does not focus on peace as inner calm and tranquility at the expense of peace as reconciliation in social relations and structures. Nor does the New Testament consider peace to be the balance of self-interest between power groups regulated by an extensive legal system and maintained by military might. Such a view is part of the Roman legacy to Western culture. All too often Christianity has adopted this notion of peace when it has identified itself with a particular group or nation. The differences between the Old and New Testaments have to do rather with the way in which Jesus fulfilled the messianic expectations of the Old and the way in which shalom took shape in the church as the messianic community. These differences transform but do not eliminate the structural and social dimensions of peace understood in the Hebraic sense of *shalom.*

The messianic peace inaugurated by Jesus and characterizing the Christian community springs from Christ's sacrifice on the cross. As a mature missionary-theologian, the Apostle Paul summarizes in Ephesians 2 and 3 the "mystery" about the present age made known to him by revelation. According to the revelation of this mystery—something which had previously remained hidden from the sight and knowledge of humanity— God's intent at the present time is that His "manifold wisdom" be made known "to the rulers and authorities in heavenly realms" through the church. As made clear in the apostle's summary, he does not mean simply that the church should transmit a particular message which in some curious way will be communicated to angelic powers. God would hardly have needed such a devious route of communication with angelic hosts. The crucial issue is rather that the church now exists as the messianic community made up of both Jew and Gentile. Those who had previously been divided by an insurmountable hostility of religious, social, cultural, and political dimensions now were reconciled and participated on an equal basis in the messianic *shalom.* The community made up of former enemies is itself the message—visible as well as verbal—of God's intent in creation, as in the cross of Christ. In the Ephesians summary, reconciliation and peace between former enemies even provide the context in which both may live in "peace with God." The peace between Jew and Gentile is the realm in which the reality of peace with God may be experienced—rather than a possible secondary and derivative consequence of a purely transcendent peace with God. The messianic peace encompasses both the reconciliation of enemies on the social level as well as the common access to the presence of God.

Contrary to several strands in the Old testament expectations as well as among the Jewish people of the first century, Jesus as the Messiah made peace by suffering and death, rather than by righteous vengeance and the domination of the enemies of God's people. "But now in Christ Jesus you who once were far away have been brought near through the blood of Christ. For he himself is our peace, who has made the two one and has destroyed the barrier. . . . His purpose was to create in himself one new man out of the two, thus making peace, and in this one body to reconcile both of them to God through the cross, by which he put to death their hostility" (Ephesians 2:13 ff., NIV). The peace established by Jesus as the Messiah thus retains and even goes beyond the Hebraic understanding of shalom as including the social relations among God's people and between the people and God. It includes the realization of reconciliation and community unattainable by human efforts and therefore relegated to a utopian future age. What had been considered utopian had now through the cross become present reality.

Traditional doctrines of the atonement have usually focused on the language of sacrifice and have understood the work of Christ for the salvation of humankind above all in relation to His death on the cross. Whether of Anselmic or Abelardian learnings, whether explaining Christ's death on the cross as a ransom paid to the devil or as a demonstration of His power over the evil one, and whatever else their strengths or weaknesses, the classic understandings of the atonement have overlooked or neglected any direct relation between the crucifixion and the social reality of the messianic peace. They have focused rather on the enmity between the sinful or guilty soul and God, thus abstracting from both the social reality of sin as well as of reconciliation.

The language of Paul's summary however emphasizes that the work of Christ inherently means the making of peace between human enemies as well as providing their common access to God. Peacemaking between enemies thus belongs fundamentally to the death and resurrection of Jesus Christ—not only to Christian social ethics once the enmity with God has been overcome. This making of peace includes both a destructive and a constructive action.

By His death on the cross, Jesus "has destroyed the barrier, the dividing wall of hostility, by abolishing in his flesh the law with its commandments and regulations" (Ephesians 2:14 f., NIV). Peacemaking in the sense of the biblical shalom means first of all negation of whatever causes division and hostility. It begins at the point of offense in the situation of conflict and confronts that offense rather than simply calling for greater toleration or balancing of one offense against another. The offense between Jew and Gentile was founded on "the law with its commandments and regulations." What had originally been given to the Jewish people as a part of God's covenant with His people had become a means of perpetuating and justifying division from and enmity with the Gentiles. The uniqueness of Jewish existence and of its relation to God was defined in such a way that it meant division from and enmity with the Gentiles. This division and hostility continued to shape the mood and actions of many early Christians—even though contrary to the leading of the Holy Spirit as recounted in Acts. But as Paul rightly insists, the fulfillment of the messianic peace in the Christian community means the destruction of the occasion for enmity and prejudice. The crucifixion of Jesus as the representative of God's chosen people means that He has taken the initiative to destroy the barrier between His people and their enemies rather than compelling the outsiders to submit to the spiritual and social domination of His people, or rather than simply leaving them outside the scope of His peace. In solidarity with Jesus, Jewish Christians were thus freed to die to the presumed necessity of finding their identity in a religious, social, and cultural reality which ratified enmity with all those outside their own ethnic group.

Nothing less than the cross of the Messiah could overcome a hostility as profound and pervasive as that between Jew and Gentile. In situations of radical enmity, the conflict may be overcome only by the elimination or defeat of the enemy. The elimination of the enemy, whether in personal or social conflict as experienced on the human level, however, rules out any reconciliation between the opposing parties. The defeat of the enemy in such conflict situations only reinforces the resentment on the part of the defeated and relegates him to the status of subjugated or second-class citizen in relation to the victor. The defeat of the enemy only reinforces, on the part of the victor, his own personal or social identity, now further strengthened by the experience of having conquered the one who threatened that identity. These examples may serve as partial analogies to the way in which only the death of Jesus on the cross could overcome the hostility between Jew and Gentile. "Through the cross" this conflict was destroyed without relegating the Gentiles to second-class citizenship in the messianic community. "Through the cross" the hostility was defeated without reinforcing the kind of Jewish existence which necessarily implied enmity with the Gentiles or spiritual or political subjugation to the Jews.

The making of peace and the reconciliation of former enemies has a constructive side. In destroying the barrier of hostility, Jesus' purpose "was to create in Himself one new man out of the two, thus making peace." This constructive side confirms the Hebraic understanding of shalom which goes beyond mere absence of conflict to a reordering and restructuring of social relations between former enemies and between them and God. In this aspect of making peace the Messiah is the representative of a new humanity. He is the new "image of God" who incarnates a human identity in which reconciliation and peace rather than strife and division become a visible and social reality. Paul's language here is rooted in the creation account, but now oriented around the new creation in the Person and corporate existence of the Messiah. Both Jew and Gentile are given a new basis for existence. Rather than perpetuating their uniqueness as experienced and defined over against each other, they are granted a new common existence in Christ. The new humanity created by the Messiah is His own corporate existence, the messianic community in which hostilities are overcome and former enemies live in peace. The messianic peace thus includes a change of attitude, but also an equally fundamental restructuring of social realities in the messianic community. National, racial, class, and cultural division and enmity are replaced by a peace which overcomes such divisions and reflects the unity of humankind in Jesus Christ.

The creation of a new corporate existence in which hostility and conflict give way to a new social and religious identity does not however amount to a kind of cosmopolitan universalism, in which the "Gentiles" gain the upper hand. The new community in which the messianic peace takes on social reality is not the realization of a humanistic universalism, but the participation of former enemies in the particular corporate existence of the Messiah. The Apostle Paul can therefore speak of Gentiles, Jews, and "the church of God" (1 Corinthians 10). Nor does the fulfillment of the messianic shalom provide a rationale for the elaboration and imposition of a "Christian culture" upon all. The peace of the messianic community is a dynamic rather than a static reality which begins ever anew at the points of offense and hostility between conflicting peoples with the message of reconciliation between themselves and God. As such, the messianic community by its corporate and social existence points toward the final peace and reconciliation of all creatures, which God will establish in His name (Colossians 1).

In addition to the continuity with the Hebraic vision of peace and the Pauline summary of Christ's work on the cross as reconciliation between former enemies, the broader testimony of the New Testament speaks for the structural and social dimensions of the messianic peace. In the messianic community, peace and reconciliation include the creation of new relations between men and women, relations which had been marked by alienation and structures of domination since the fall as described in Genesis. Shalom means a new social and structural relation of mutual service between men and women rather than hostility or domination based on sexual difference. The work of Christ similarly transformed the structure of relations between slaves and masters in the messianic community. Even though the legal and economic structures which perpetuated the "institution" of slavery continued in the broader society, the social reality of these relations began to take on the shape of shalom in the messianic community (Philemon, 1 Corinthians, Ephesians).

The social dimensions of the messianic peace also extend to the economic area, where wealth becomes another form of power which engenders hostility, oppression, and conflict. The Apostle Paul, who proclaimed the gospel of peace between Jew and Gentile, also helped organize the redistribution of material resources between

Jewish and Gentile Christians. Not only was this redistribution to respond to the particular material needs under which Jewish Christians suffered, but it was to be carried out according to the "rule of equality" (2 Corinthians 8). Far from being limited to a subjective attitude about the charitable sharing of excess wealth, the collection organized by Paul was a means of making the final equality between former enemies part of the messianic peace. Even though the economic inequalities and divisions of the broader society continued to engender hostility and conflict, the church began to live out this dimension of reconciliation and peace. In making material sharing according to the "rule of equality" part of the gospel of peace, the Apostle Paul continued the tradition of the early Jerusalem Christians who had "all things in common."

The gospel of peace thus integrally belongs to the good news about Jesus Christ. The message of peace means that through no merit of our own, we are in Christ reconciled to our enemies and called to participate in the social realities of a new community where old structures of personal, social, and economic hostility are replaced by those of reconciliation. In this sense the gospel of peace is a social gospel. It differs from other social gospels, however, which would attempt to establish peace and overcome conflict by domination and power rather than by inviting men and women to participation in the messianic community. The gospel of peace is also the proclamation of a present reality which has begun to take shape in a world characterized by strife, injustice, and power struggles—not simply a utopian vision of a desirable future. Finally the gospel of peace is both a message and a corporate existence. The credibility of the message will therefore depend in large measure upon the community which proclaims it.

Understood as part of the gospel of peace, several New Testament passages usually cited as support for an almost exclusively individual and subjective understanding of reconciliation and peace with God, in fact express a more comprehensive perspective. For example, most translations of 2 Corinthians 5 encourage an understanding of God's reconciling work in Christ limited to an inner and personal transformation. Instead of the familiar "if anyone is in Christ, he is a new creature" (or an equivalent rendering), a more accurate translation of verse 17 would read "therefore, if anyone is in Christ, (there is a) new creation—the old has gone, behold the new has come." Through reconciliation in Christ there is thus a whole new perspective, a whole new way of looking at the world. Rather than others being judged from the worldly perspective of status, nationality, culture, class, gender, or race, they are now seen as befits their common participation "in Christ." Reconciliation thus means both peace with God as well as with those previously considered enemies. Another example is the familiar opening verse of Romans 5. "Therefore, since we have been justified through faith, we have peace with God through our Lord Jesus Christ." Even though the immediate context of Romans 5:1 does not explicitly refer to the social dimensions of shalom, it does not exclude them either, particularly in view of the Hebraic understanding of shalom which includes both spiritual and social reconciliation. Moreover the broader setting of Romans 5 has to do with the theological foundations of the gospel addressed to both Jew and Gentile. Just as the shalom of the messianic community may not be reduced to a purely social reality, so this social dimension may not be excluded from the peace with God incarnate in Jesus Christ.

A renewed vision of the gospel of peace as an integral part of the good news of Jesus Christ would have far-reaching consequences for missionary thought and practice. It would mean a theological reorientation with respect to central, traditional, doctrinal formulations which have not been foundationally shaped by the social dimensions of the good news. It would mean an understanding of the Apostle Paul as a peacemaker, continuing the teaching of Jesus on peace as well as His reconciling way of the cross in the cities of the Roman Empire. It would mean an extension of the missionary proclamation in our time to include the messianic peace addressed to situations of enmity and injustice. It would mean giving priority to theological and missionary efforts which focus on points of conflict and reconciliation rather than reinforcing or totally undergirding given social and economic conflicts and enmity. It would mean the renewal of the church as a messianic community whose basis for existence derives not from national, ethnic, or cultural givens, but from an ever new corporate identity in Christ. To all of this and more we are called and freed by the "good news of peace through Jesus Christ."

2

THE SEARCH FOR A BIBLICAL PEACE TESTIMONY

Sjouke Voolstra

Why do the Historic Peace Churches (and, fortunately, some other Christians) persist in raising questions about the biblical basis for the peace witness? Is it merely an indication of academic curiosity? No, I believe it is more likely because of a frightening realization that the traditional bases for our peace testimony are constantly being challenged by the fast changing times and the shifting spirit of the age. The matter-of-course way and the self-evident attitude with which the Mennonites have explained their views on questions of nonresistance and relationship to the world, and in particular the state—as based on the traditional biblical texts and the Anabaptist heritage—have become an urgent agenda. This does not mean that the traditional arguments were not valid in their given historical context, but that these traditional answers will only have truth if they address the questions of today. The questions of our time are indeed different ones than those of four hundred and fifty, one hundred, or even twenty years ago.

This insecurity concerning the biblical basis of our peace witness can be understood as a part of the fundamental identity crisis of the whole Christian church in the affluent, capitalist West. There is a new awareness of the tension between the identity of the church and its significance in society. Is the church turning out only words, not deeds? Do the words produce action and are they accompanied by changed behavior in the church itself? Many accuse the church of having shown a negative rather than a positive relevancy in the past. Is it not high time that we spotlight the church's relevancy to social, political, and cultural dimensions of a fast changing world, and not only to the personal dimension?

How should this happen? Because millions cry for justice, peace, and freedom, the church is not allowed to be irrelevant. However, there is much confusion on how the church can serve the cause of humanity in this world. Some careful rethinking must be done. Since the church's cause is the cause of faith in the God of Israel, the Father of Jesus Christ, then theological rethinking of the biblical tradition is the first requirement. A better theology is itself a first step to a better strategy.

I

This essay does not intend to enumerate a series of favorite biblical texts, prooftexting the Bible on the matter of peace. The focus is rather on presuppositions of our peace witness which affect the practice of peace in our churches. These presuppositions are not merely theological. Peace is not the logical result of an intellectual effort. Peace is above all a way of life, praxis, obedience to and confidence in Christ who is the Prince of Peace. But, on the other side, this commitment must not be reduced by a too narrowly understood biblical interpretation of peace. In order to free the concept of peace from its ahistorical, individualized features, a biblically sound interpretation must go through at least two phases in order to answer the questions of today.

1. We analyze the way in which the biblical texts have had certain effects on the course of history, and can be understood as interpretations of and reactions to particular historical situations. This quest for sociopolitically oriented hermeneutics can be useful in determining how the biblical tradition regarding the peace witness can be realized in our time.

2. We analyze the ways in which the *church* should deal with the questions of peace. This is a request for strategy and for relevancy of the church to society today.

Each of these analyses presupposes the other. The one cannot lead to fruitful study without the other. Therefore a peace theology must be developed in communication with other scholarly studies; a peace theology can become a model of cooperative, interdisciplinary study.

One of the basic questions at the root of this comprehensive task is: What is our relation to God and our responsibility to our world, wherein God's kingdom of peace and justice is to be established and manifested by His people? This question leads to a second one: How can the church form a new fruitbearing relationship between faith and sociopolitical action? An adequate peace theology cannot ignore these questions, because the question of our day to the church is concerned with the sociopolitical dimension of conversion—metanoia. What is the meaning of the new life in God's kingdom in an as yet unsaved world? The spirit of Christ is already at work in the old world, in a revolutionary way in and outside the church. But the Spirit struggles against counter-revolutionary powers of that world which have set up a strong resistance. The church only finds her true identity when she is at work as a fellowship of the Spirit in a completely unique and revolutionary way in the old world. The church's relevancy grows from and is determined by this sharing in and partaking of the Spirit's work.

If peace churches take seriously their peace witness, they will, in the first place, have to face squarely the questions of peace and justice today in the light of the sociopolitical interpretation of the biblical testimony. Christ is and remains the foundation for the peace He brought, the peace He is and will work out through us as His obedient followers. But this peace is not a philosophical idea afloat somewhere above historical reality that can be translated into reality by our human ingenuity. In Christ, God Himself has translated His word into human historical reality. This reality should therefore be interpreted from the perspective of God's statesmanship—the kingdom of God. A theology of the kingdom of God, which consists of peace and justice, must be the starting point for a theology of peace because God must deal with a person in his historical situation.

The message of the eighth-century prophets such as Amos and Isaiah is no less "physical and temporary" than it is "spiritual and eternal." The prophets are referring primarily to social and political events that were about to happen in their time. In Jesus also the eternal, spiritual ruling presence of God broke into human, temporal, finite, historical reality, though in a new and definitive way. God's peace is not what we are used to calling "religious," reduced to our existence as persons or the church. God's peace has to do with universal world history. History is one complex process, and in this process we discern the activity of God. The basis of our discernment is the life, death, and resurrection of Jesus, and the promise of the fulfilment of all things in Him. The only way to know the will of God, to interpret His purposes, and therefore understand history is through reflection on Scripture in the context of obedient participation in the concerns and struggles of our contemporary history. We should emphasize more this hermeneutical approach to Scripture, instead of reading the Bible as an illustration of our personal feelings, experiences, and beliefs. This approach is a corrective to an uncritical fundamentalism which always tends to provide an ideology for maintaining the status quo. Seeking the kingdom of God and His righteousness (Matthew 6:33) is fundamental, for the kingdom liberates us from self-centered concern and enables us to love God, neighbor, and the enemy. Self- or group-interest takes a backseat, as do pseudo-psychological interpretations of personal salvation, for these are now seen as denials of God's rule and as forms of escape from engagement within history. The kingdom of God is directly related to issues affecting man in society. The kingdom is profoundly political, though its orientation, its means, its criteria, and its goals are "not of this world." God's peace is therefore a historical, sociopolitical reality that would change the old order from inside out until all power in heaven and on earth be given to the firstborn of the new order.

For too long, the churches have felt that it was their task to be the keepers of order in an unregenerate world. The Dutch Doopsegezinden (Mennonites), for example, have for too long felt their task in the world was to be individually responsible to the established order. For too long, Mennonites, through the use of a dualistic ethic, have thought they could give a permanent example of purity to an unregenerate world. Today our challenge is to relate to the world in a way determined not by individuals but by the church. The church lives as a redeemed world within an unredeemed world, in the midst of confrontation and conflict, and seeks neither conformity nor separation. The love of God resists attack from the forces of the old and does not limit itself only to the peace and well-being of God's own people. The church is on the front lines of the battle for peace and justice.

II

In order to comprehend the full content of biblical peace we must also not forget to read the Old Testament. Mennonites have too often limited themselves to the New Testament and considered the Old Testament a collection of saintly biographies. Christ's message of the kingdom is continually threatened with becoming individualized and spiritualized if it has no roots in the Old Testament. It is surprising how seldom serious readers of the Sermon on the Mount have taken note of one comment of Jesus, "Think not that I have come to abolish the law and the prophets; I have come not to abolish them but to fulfill them" (Matthew 5:17).

In order to identify the social relevance of biblical peace it is necessary to look at the Old Testament idea of peace (shalom) more closely. One cannot build a peace theology by pointing out the idea of peace in the Bible separately from its historical context and ignoring the influence these words have had during the course of history in their various interpretations. Therefore, the following search for the meaning of the word peace in the Old Testament can only be the starting point for theological thinking through the full volume of God's dealing with His people in history. The study of the concept of shalom has already proven itself as such a starting point during the sixties when the question of the political and social relevancy of the church arose anew. The inquiry into the Old Testament peace principle formed an important contribution to the new thought regarding peace in the last decades in Europe.

Shalom originally had no political meaning or military connotation as the opposite of war. If it does occur within this setting it is only in a much broader context which I would like to sketch briefly.

1. Shalom includes social justice: the protection of widows, orphans, and society's dependents; the struggle against exploitation and oppression; the protection of life and property; and the human treatment of slaves and servants. But any tendency in the Old Testament toward social revolution is out of the question. The social structures of Old Testament times were too sound and solid for such a radical change. Also, the political and cultural presuppositions of that society were different from those of the present time. But would not the call for social justice sound revolutionary to the ears of some groups in all times?

2. Parallel to the social aspect of shalom is the process of thinking and learning in the framework of just laws

and wisdom. Shalom can only exist where justice rules, where justice is spoken in the courts and practiced by the people. In the same way wisdom must be the content of education and nurture in order for shalom to exist. We can assume that our human endeavor on behalf of the law of nations as well as the search for a true basis for peace education derives from the concept of shalom.

3. Nature itself is included in shalom. Shalom is expressed in fertility and excess. The analytical, objective thinking of the empirical sciences has, however, brought about an alienation between man and nature so that the primeval unity of nature and peace has disappeared. Problems relating to our natural environment, pollution, radioactivity, and unnatural food production open our eyes afresh to this dimension of shalom.

4. Of course, shalom is most closely bound up with the faith of Israel. It is above all a religious concept, as well as a sociopolitical one. How one envisions peace is largely determined by one's religious background and worldview. The distinctive element of this religious dimension of shalom lies in the believer's conviction that the achievement of a truly peaceful situation is something beyond human ability. One expects peace ultimately from God. This conviction appears in direct proportion to man's desperate strivings for peace. The quality of God's shalom is eternally different from man's desire for peace.

These four dimensions of the peace concept in the Old Testament belong together. This fourfold peace is basically one and the same, an indivisible unit. Any disturbance in any one of these four areas is necessarily destructive of peace in the other sectors. This comprehensive thinking has been lost in our day, but it is not antiquated. On the contrary, for the sake of the future of this world, it should become the incentive for bringing together those disciplines which have become alienated.

If we do not just evaluate the wealth of the Old Testament idea of peace, the New Testament concept of peace is also impoverished. We must not forget that for Jesus, faith had a clearly stated sociopolitical dimension. He referred to the social questions of the major prophets in His attack on the faithlessness and failure to keep the covenant in His time. He protested the reduction of social justice to the giving of a pittance and the reduction of righteousness to small deeds of mercy. Jesus told His disciples, "For I tell you, unless your righteousness exceeds that of the scribes and Pharisees, you will never enter the kingdom of heaven" (Matthew 5:20). Jesus places righteousness before religious requirements or ritual, just as the prophets do. Peace is the result of a righteousness which exceeds the righteousness of the old forms. This peace is composed of wholeness, health, and well-being and grows out of brotherly love, the readiness to serve and to sacrifice.

The last level of the biblical concept of peace in the New Testament is based on the Old Testament framework of thought. Jesus is the One who fulfills the promises. At the same time, however, the New Testament is a continuation and a specific interpretation of certain Old Testament thought patterns, such as when it speaks of the life of Jesus as God's strength in weakness, even in suffering. This paradox is not passivity or the relinquishing of power. Rather, in order to make righteousness and peace manifest in the world another kind of power is needed. This power is with a person who implicitly keeps faith in the covenant that the God of Israel makes with all people, even to the point of suffering and in doing so causes peace and justice to flourish around him. It is the powerful incentive given by God's Spirit.

III

The deepening of the concept of peace, rooted in the Old Testament and brought into being by Jesus, has given a broader orientation to the peace question in the last decades. Peace can no longer be understood exclusively as the antithesis of war. Peace work before World War II was largely anti-militaristic in emphasis. In our time we have discovered that militarism is only the tip of the iceberg, and we have realized, though still imperfectly, that it is a consolidation of injustices in which we—consciously or unconsciously, willingly or unwillingly—have participated. A rather defensive, anti-militaristic pacifism must find a more rounded, "aggressive" approach to the power structures that block the road to peace. This underscores the question of how this can be done without betraying our obedience to the suffering Lord and without conforming to society.

New attention has also been paid to the study of the way Jesus walked in obedience to God who established in His own unique way peace and justice on earth. Here there has been a noticeable shift from the initial insight that described Jesus' nonresistance as only passivity. We now realize that Jesus' nonresistance was an outstanding example of the activity of God's struggle for peace. Jesus' nonresistance was an intrinsic part of God's strategy for peace in His attack on the old order. Nonresistance is thus no longer merely an ahistorical ethical principle. Christians should not relate to a principle (traditionally tolerated by their government), but to a historical, incarnated, sociopolitically relevant reality, Christ the risen

One Himself. Our stance therefore cannot be determined by an ahistorical principle such as nonresistance, interpreted as merely passivity and noninvolvement in history, but by the historical, living reality of a compassionate Christ. Christ is the announcement and fulfillment of God's kingdom which consists of *shalom* and *zedeka* (peace and justice). We should pray for a new creative act of civil disobedience, similar to the sixteenth-century believer's baptism, as an attack on the structural (economic) causes of war, poverty, injustice, and oppression in our world.

In this rediscovery of the full meaning of biblical shalom, it is important to see that it primarily takes form in the church. What peace is becomes concretely apparent in a special and exemplary way of living together. The Gospels and the Epistles describe this process, for they spring from church life itself. They can also be read as ongoing corrections to the way in which these churches in their own specific situations strayed from the original meaning of Jesus. Peace, Christ, and the church have gradually become united in the endeavor toward a new peace theology in the last decades. Biblical peace should primarily be communicated to the world through the church which lives of the Spirit. This understanding sets totally new, radical standards for the character of the body called the church, and many deepen the chasm between the world and Christian understanding of peace. Inevitably conflict will result with the unregenerate world. This ongoing creative conflict with the old order is a prerequisite of the peace church.

Those in the Anabaptist-Mennonite tradition have a peculiar assignment in the search for a biblically based peace theology. They will need to state clearly that the local gathering of committed believers in community is the primary expression of the reality of the peace of Christ and the primary means of communicating this peace to the world. Therefore they have to free themselves from individualism and a primarily individualistic and ahistorical interpretation of Scripture. In full solidarity with each other, the peace churches need to make clear that the witness of the church is reduced if the church is not involved in the struggle for peace and justice in our time.

We can learn from the many community-oriented groups within the various traditions which consider peace as the organizing principle of the church. Generally, authentic peace is experienced by the poor, small, and powerless; not by the rich, powerful, and well-established people. Therefore, we shall have to reconsider our wealth and particularly our concepts of private property and free enterprise which may be some of the greatest obstacles to peace. The traditional, closed doors of the church must be opened to the cries for justice and peace from the millions of "outsiders." Only when we, in answer to this call for peace and justice, dare to lose our traditional identity, will we find a new identity in the form of new fellowships.

The search for a peace theology becomes an academic question unless it is practiced as a peace witness in the church. A peace theology must be subservient to the building up and restoration of new peace churches; it must also have a missionary zeal. Theory and practice, identity and relevance, cannot be separated. The search for a peace theology begins in churches which are involved in historical reality and the struggle for peace and justice in the world.

3

SHALOM IS THE MISSION

James E. Metzler

The term "shalom" is not foreign to most of us. Unfortunately, it isn't very meaningful either. It may cause you to recall the peace marches of a decade ago or to picture two Jewish friends clinging to an element of their tradition. But for me, shalom has become a most exciting concept: the freshest approach to the Scriptures and the most dynamic guide for our life and witness today.[1]

Throughout the biblical message, from Genesis to Revelation, no term better describes God's vision for His creation than the concept of shalom. It is a fundamental and comprehensive term, used in every period of the history of God's people. Though used as a common greeting in everyday life, it was used also by the prophets to portray their wildest dreams of the good life. Walter Brueggemann describes shalom as:

The central vision of world history in the Bible ... that all of creation is one, every creature in community with every other, living in harmony and security toward the joy and well-being of every other creature ... it bears tremendous freight, the freight of a dream of God which resists all our tendencies to division, hostility, fear, drivenness and misery.[2]

Unfortunately most Bible translators have failed to capture shalom's rich meaning. They have usually translated it simply as "peace," but rarely does the original setting relate to anything near the narrow confines of our present word "peace."[3] Hebrew scholars say that the word is so inclusive that only the specific setting can indicate how each usage should be translated.

The basic meaning of shalom is wholeness, which includes the ideas of uninjuredness, totality or completeness, well-being, prosperity, harmony, and having a common will and a mutual responsibility. It is used as a companion word with—and sometimes as a synonym for— the terms "blessing," "salvation," "righteousness," and "justice." Shalom depicts the relationship that God establishes and intends for humanity with Himself, other humans, and nature. It relates to communion and fulfillment, where the claims and needs of each individual-in-community are satisfied. It is clearly a gift of God and is directly related to His rule and power. In this essay I will attempt to outline the biblical theme of shalom, then look at how we have presented shalom in mission, and finally project a new vision and model.

I

First, the biblical theme needs examination. In the tribal setting of early biblical history, shalom was largely a social term picturing the harmony and well-being of the family and tribe. It referred to identity, solidarity, and security within one's group; any arrival or departure affected the shalom in an organic way. To wish another "shalom" became equated with blessing, while anything anti-shalom was seen as evil. Whenever the shalom was broken, either vengeance or restitution was needed to restore the balance required for shalom.

As societies developed, community came to be founded more on law than kinship, so that treaties (covenants) became necessary to create and maintain shalom. Wherever one went, a person was either protected by an old covenant or made a new one. All life was viewed as being held together by these agreements to live in "one-will" with others (the Hebrew concept of love). This was the primary reality that Yahweh chose to symbolize His relationship with His people. The Mosaic covenant was based on God having delivered His people from their anti-shalom situation of bondage, and now was relating to them in an open-ended, dynamic kingship. More and more, shalom was seen to be possible only in this relationship with God, which recognized no other gods or powers but Him. Worship was a celebration of this political allegiance to Yahweh alone.

Thus very early in redemption history, shalom indicated God's movement from chaos and bondage into orderliness and freedom; however, it was a relationship that was grounded in His people's response, trust, and faithfulness. Instead of viewing the Israelites' journey to Canaan (as well as the period of the judges) as being the dark ages, we really should see this period as the Old Testament's golden age when God's rule among His people was most dynamic and direct.

What we have often called the golden age, with it's imperialism, dynasties, and temple should be seen as the period of Israel's rebellion—as Samuel and all the Yahwistic prophets declared it to be. Israel wanted to capture, freeze, and institutionalize something that could never be, seeking to be like "the nations." The institutions of empire, kingship, and religion were all viewed as anti-shalom, and were denounced and opposed by the true prophets. They were all part of a law-and-order system, supported by the civil-religion court prophets, which produced a false shalom based on force and violence. The faithful prophets declared that there is no shalom apart from faithfulness to Yahweh's covenant, seen in economic justice and right living.

At this point the prophets began to dream of a day when God would again be related to His people, after these structures of false shalom were destroyed. Repeatedly they spoke of a new *covenant of shalom* which God would make with His people, reflecting back to the Garden of Eden (Ezekiel 36:35; 37:26, 27). All creation will be renewed in wholeness and harmony, as God teaches us His ways and we walk in His paths (Isaiah 2:2-4; Micah 4:1-4). But second Isaiah realized that this would be possible only through forgiveness, which restores the balance necessary for shalom through redemptive suffering rather than vengeance, as modeled by the servant of Yahweh.

This is precisely what Jesus did in His life and death. To view Jesus' ministry through the eyes of shalom makes it seem alive in an exciting way. His preaching focused on announcing the kingdom, the new day of God's rule among His people, which is the basis for shalom. His extensive healing attacked the forces of chaos and coercion, bringing deliverance, order, and wholeness through response and commitment.

Jesus' ministry was focused on the creation of shalom communities, forming a new people to live together under God's rule. Politically and economically, the Jesus movement parallels the wilderness experience. His "come and follow" invitation called forth bands of followers who joined in "one-will" community. John 11:48-50 shows the false shalom of the court prophets chosen in contrast to the true shalom, which Jesus grounded on the prophetic word of witness in contrast to the coercive force of the sword (John 18:36, 37).

The powers of forgiveness and freedom released by Christ's death and resurrection are seen in the New Testament as the foundation of our shalom.[4] In Ephesians 2, Paul says that shalom is experienced as people of all races are joined in community under Christ's lordship—and this he identified as salvation! Jesus breaks down the walls of hostility, alienation, and individualism, creating one new humanity in Himself of people who covenant together to follow God.

For Paul, the meaning of being saved or being "in Christ" was primarily that of becoming a member of this shalom community of Jesus. The theme of shalom is so essential in the New Testament that in several places God is called the God of shalom, and the gospel is referred to as the good news of shalom. Apparently no other descriptive term is sufficiently comprehensive to describe the gospel, only shalom!

II

If shalom best describes God's will and intention for His people, and if the gospel is the good news of a new covenant of shalom, then shalom should be a very common and vital term for missions. It should be utilized as a principal guide in fulfilling every aspect of our commission, prescribing both the message and the means of our mission, especially among people who have taken a courageous stance for peace and brotherhood through the centuries! However, my readings, observations, and experience indicate that this is far from the case! It would seem that most Mennonite missionaries have only given verbal assent to an Anabaptist view of salvation, saying that peace is at the heart of the gospel. But either it wasn't nearly as central as had been thought, or it wasn't the gospel of Christ that our followers received, for Mennonites have largely failed to reproduce the Anabaptist peace witness, or any recognizable part of the shalom vision, in their missions.

It is not that no one really tried to share concerns for nonresistance, but all these efforts have been greatly compromised by a theology of salvation and a model of missions that could not produce or support a shalom community. The impossible has been tried: holding to an Anabaptist ethic while adopting Protestant understandings of the gospel and methods of evangelism. We have continued reading the Sermon on the Mount, but increasingly we have seen it only relate to the individual and not to a group ethic. Our missions have been so influenced by others that it is very difficult to find any way in which our texts and reports of missions in the past are Mennonite other than in name!

This is especially sad because of the issues and needs in our world and church today. In many places, Christians are caught in the tension between two extremes: the law-and-order violence of the right-wing imperialists, and the deliverance-through-revolution violence of the left-wing liberationists. The options are seen as choosing one of these kinds of violence or quietistic withdrawal. Jesus showed that neither of these approaches are satisfactory, but are substitutes for the shalom which He seeks. All missions and missionaries are caught up in these polarizations and divided between these positions. Christians desperately need a radically different model, a third option which will allow God to produce true shalom in their midst.

I am convinced that evangelistic rallies and Sunday preaching services are not an adequate foundation for the stance in life we are envisioning. The religious life-together for most Protestants is like a Sunday morning club meeting. It is an hour to withdraw from the real world of the secular into a sacred place to take care of the past (our sins) and secure the future (salvation), plus a bit of inspiration and comradeship for the present. All this depends mainly on the pastor-priest, who has been well trained to supply all the congregational needs and to fulfill the week's religious duties of his people in one brief hour.

That such a model of Christianity has been universalized through stereotyped missions is bad enough. But that Mennonites should have substituted their heritage for this—and gone to the ends of the world to reproduce such bland religiosity—is beyond explanation! The picture of a professional missionary gathering his little flock around himself shows how well we've learned from Protestant missions, reproducing mission board mentalities at home and soul-saving emphases overseas.

One of the greatest impressions my fourteen years in Asia has left with me is the crucial importance of models in missions. A serious block in the development of the younger churches has been a lack of adequate models. The modern missionary movement has identified the primary task of the church as evangelism. Doing mission activities—especially preaching—is the only way they know to carry out their task. Many missionaries feel that evangelism is the first, last, and only vital role that they can fill, and if evangelism is the only concern of the missionaries, then that is all the young church does or knows to do. That *is* Christianity according to the only models they've seen!

I have observed missions still engaged almost solely in "church planting" after forty or sixty years of work in one area. They insist that when the local church is grown and mature enough, it will develop its own fuller expression of faith and life. But it appears that normally a church group will go no further than the example which the missionaries have lived. If shalom has not been a part of evangelism, neither will it become a part of congregational life.

The model of Christian living that Protestant missions have left does not create the community or require the commitment which our ethical stance of discipleship and this vision of shalom demands. The gospel which people see in our own lifestyles, values, methods, and spirit will likely be the only gospel they will receive and follow. It is not enough to say that people have accepted Christ; we must always ask "whose Christ" have they seen or "which Christ" do they know.

The example of Jesus clearly shows that if we want disciples, we must first be disciples and call for disciples. If our understanding of the gospel includes a nonviolent way of life, then no one will accept that gospel without receiving God's call to live as Jesus lived. If salvation is living in shalom, then we will allow no false hope that one can be saved apart from entering into a covenant relationship with God's people. Pacifism is not something that we hope new believers will come to see as a special call later on; it is *the way of life* to which they are being called (1 Peter 2:21; 3:9). Unfortunately, it took me fourteen years to reach this understanding of what the gospel and mission is all about!

III

With this background of the church's record in reproducing communities of shalom I would like to project a new vision of the biblical shalom. I believe that we need to begin with a new and firm affirmation that shalom is the will of God for all humanity. Many seem to have taken the Bible's recognition of war and coercion as continuing evidence of human sin and demonic forces to mean that violence is therefore God's will for the present. Certain views of eschatology have been influential in changing our view of our mission and message. We need a fresh awareness of the testimony proclaimed by the great salvation texts of the Scriptures: God wants shalom to be established *now* among all peoples!

From the disruption of shalom in the Garden of Eden to its total renewal in the New Jerusalem, the objective of all God's work is the recovery of shalom in His creation. All redemptive history points to the fact that God yearns for shalom. He *is* the God of shalom—so much so that any shalom-lover is identified as being godlike. That which seeks to reestablish and promote His shalom on earth is mission.

Such a theology of missions will be comprehensive. No

aspect of life is beyond the concern of shalom. It encompasses the whole person and the whole community. It emphasizes that Christianity is essentially relational. There are sacraments and rituals, creeds and dogma, morals and piety, but none of these are of its essence. The Christian life is a relationship, and spirituality is measured in terms of faithfulness in a covenanted life of discipleship. It is the ordering of our lives according to the prophets' vision of God dwelling in our midst.

With shalom as the measuring stick, the personhood of every individual will be uplifted. People alone have value and are sacred; neither tradition nor institutions nor possessions can be allowed to have more importance than people. Once more, salvation will be seen as the restoration of people-in-community. This must be seen as one of the greatest impacts of Christ's life and teaching.

In this regard, Jesus' instructions to the seventy on how to do mission work has new meaning for us today (Luke 10:1-12). Christ's view of evangelism is a matter of meeting people where they are and offering shalom, extending God's kingdom by inviting others to join us in living according to His ordering. In this passage, Jesus first emphasized a few details to set the right stage, spirit, and self-image. He pointed out that there is lots of work but few workers, that mission originates with the Lord Himself, and that workers go out as lambs among wolves. By telling them not to take any extra materials, He created a sense of dependency and vulnerability. Their message was to be embodied in one word: "Shalom." He outlined a simple three-step program for wherever their extended shalom was accepted: eat, heal, and speak.

The first step of eating in people's homes is a picture of identification with the people to whom they would go.

Jesus wanted them to foster a relationship of trust and mutuality, creating an atmosphere of openness and intimacy which will make real covenant a possibility. Second, they were to engage in servant ministries as needed. This continued Christ's own ministry to demonstrate and utilize God's power and presence, bringing wholeness and well-being into their midst. Only then were they ready for the third step of preaching, to explain this new experience as God's-kingdom-awaiting-your-response. Only after the listeners had seen and felt the shalom of God's rule would they be ready for the welcome offer to join and yield allegiance to Him. That's the gospel as good news!

This model of mission given by Jesus is so profoundly simple that I have seldom heard it taken seriously. One wonders if an entire textbook on missions could define and outline our task more clearly and fully. The disciples were taught that mission is simply extending the offer to live together in a covenant-of-shalom relationship.

For Jesus and His followers, this meant that physical needs and economic issues must be faced. As in the ancient days, the shalom of the group should be thick enough to feel! When Jesus spoke of salvation, He spoke of the forgiveness of debts, jubilee, and mutuality. His material promises were given in the context of shalom covenants; Mark 10:28-31 finds fulfillment in Acts 4:32-35. The prophets' vision of prosperity and security were interpreted as God's people giving, sharing, and trusting in the new jubilee spirit of the kingdom.

I know from experience that Jesus' economics create much difficulty for American missionaries. I'm not sure it is right for the typical missionary even to read Jesus' sayings such as Matthew 6:33 in most mission settings because of the false expectations it stirs. These are not promises of all getting rich like Americans, but of all having bread to eat together. We must face it: kingdom promises are only for kingdom citizens.

Christ's theme of shalom also gives direction in political issues. A critical problem of our overseas peace witness has been the reluctance of missionaries, as guests of generous and obliging heads of state, to do anything which might disturb the government. As we recapture the deliverance/freedom motif of shalom, we will see ourselves as God's messengers going to Egypt with His demand: "Let my people go!" To proclaim "Christ is Lord" is to declare freedom from every tyranny and allegiance on earth. As Jesus attacked the "peace" of Satan's strongholds (Luke 11:21), we too must denounce oppression of every form and structure.

Once more evangelism needs to be seen as a political rally: the proclamation of a new kingship. We should become aware of the political impact of worship—the giving of allegiance to God alone while rejecting all other claims for our loyalty and devotion. Evangelism is calling all people to join with us as a new people under God's rule. This fosters an image of being a grassroots movement of messianic communities rather than being an encroachment of foreign institutions and powers.

Missionaries have to take the same attitude toward their own government and nation. For many Americans that is likely the crux of the problem, especially for American Mennonites, who (like Israel after a long period of wandering) struggle with the temptation toward possessive ownership, permanent institutions, and powerful structures. Many missionaries "away from home" tend to become supernationalists. I've found that nothing reveals one's attachments quite like the thought of changing one's citizenship.

Ironically, shalom is for exiles and pilgrims. It is God's gift to those who free themselves from all earthly substitutes. It cannot be forced, bought, or manipulated. God offers it to those who, like Abraham, pull up their stakes and walk with Him. This is what Hebrews 11 calls faith: acknowledging God as Ruler by ordering our values and lifestyles accordingly.

Shalom is so risky and demanding that both the Israelites and the Galatians wanted to return to the comforting security of bondage. Yet shalom can only come in a trusting relationship and a loyal commitment both to God and to His people around us. Jesus was realistic enough to face the fact that His call to shalom inevitably disturbs the false shalom of those who are left behind or are unable to respond to God's offer. One of Jesus' frequent missionary themes was, "You will be hated by all." The Bible suggests that the more radical, simple, and childlike our experience of God's shalom, the more puny and futile the world's struggle to force and maintain its "peace" appears, and the more angry and resentful it becomes.

The guideline of shalom further indicates that missions need to be willing to follow a stance of vulnerable servanthood. It is true that the missionary era evoked great heroic sacrifices by individuals and the establishment of many service programs and centers. However, much of the service has been seen as demeaning paternalism and institutionalism. So much service has been so wrapped in "the white man's burden" and given with ulterior and conflicting motivations that very little of the spirit of Jesus has been felt in it. The image of missions has suffered tremendously throughout the world by associations with exploiters, colonialists, and oppressors, so that even much well-meaning service has been received with suspicion. We should not forget that the Roman Legionnaires and their puppet Herodians also were "serving" the people of Jesus' day.

The incarnation of God's covenant came to us in weakness and humility. Jesus took both the spirit and the stance of a servant. The vulnerability of the cross, by which He lived long before He died, was integral both to His message and to His model of mission. His genius and power were seen in creating a people through the discipling process in which He lived so openly and wholly among His followers that they could simply live with Him. Are we ready to take shalom that seriously?

IV

With this new vision of shalom, we must search for other models which will embody the cross and resurrection today. We must find true power in the loving service of our healing and freeing ministries that make people and communities whole. Jesus gave us the towel and basin as both symbols and agents of His shalom. But all our service will be ineffective if it is not accompanied with concrete and sincere identification.

Readiness to enter into shalom commitments with others requires missionaries who burn their bridges behind them. This view of the gospel calls for people who are ready to covenant in daily life for discipling and mutual accountability. It requires becoming involved in the lives of new believers in ways that assure security and well-being. Christ's own ministry of a few brief years shows that the issue is not merely the length of time spent together, but the depth of commitment to become the body of Christ wherever we are. Such authentic incarnation of the gospel is neither possible nor desirable by the old mission models we have followed.

Nearly two decades ago John H. Yoder called into question this traditional Protestant approach to missions in his booklet *As You Go.*[5] On the basis of the way missions were carried out in the Book of Acts, Yoder presented a clear and distinct option. Bands of pilgrims, migrating here and there, relating to each other in a way that demonstrates every aspect of the gospel, and living in a community that is open to every new seeker—this is the kind of mission which the New Testament describes and for which shalom is the sum and substance.

In this approach both mission and shalom are natural, spontaneous products of the Christian life. As in the New Testament, neither are seen as deliberate acts of obedience, but rather the essence of what it means to be Christian. Both mission and shalom are rooted in our being disciples—being that has meaning only in our life with God and His people.[6] Thus the compelling motivation for shalom creates a mission: the call to incarnate God's loving forgiveness and freeing reconciliation in a world of hostility. Extending and actualizing God's shalom in the world *is* our mission.

I propose the following then, as a model of mission for a shalom theology: enabling six to ten families, representing sufficient gifts and skills to supply whatever the group needs that would not be locally available, to settle in an underdeveloped place in order to fulfill the church's mission by sharing their life-together with those who wish to join them in faith and community. Such an approach blends service, development, and evangelism in a holistic shalom way. It allows us to share the resources of the "haves" with the "have nots" in a way that keeps integrity for both and promotes sound development. Such a model puts being before doing, relationship above program, person over institution, and faithfulness ahead of effectiveness.

There are a number of mission-communities in the United States today who embody something of this new direction in mission. I believe the insights and strategy of John Perkins and the Voice of Calvary (Mississippi) point to a more adequate model for a shalom theology than most of the Mennonite work in the past. I see many challenging, adaptable patterns for our overseas witness in the communities of Jubilee (Philadelphia), Sojourners (Washington), Koinonia (Georgia), and others. All these are seeking to utilize the powerful potential of community in mission.

Jeremiah sensed the relationship of shalom and mission when he appealed to his people in Babylon (29:7):

> Seek the *shalom* of the city where I have sent you into exile, and pray to the Lord on its behalf, for in its *shalom* you will find your *shalom*.

Today we can paraphrase his appeal in our life to read: "where I have sent you in mission." But would not Jeremiah point out that if we continue to fulfill our mission Jonah-style (pretending to offer shalom while actually withholding it), then for our children the text may well stand as written! For it is in giving that we receive; it is in seeking shalom for others that we find it for ourselves. Shalom is the mission!

4

A CALL FOR EVANGELICAL NONVIOLENCE[1]

Ronald J. Sider

To discuss nonviolence today seems insane. We dare not cry peace, for there is no peace on earth today—and there shouldn't be any. Our planet is lurching toward a nuclear Armageddon. The superpowers are armed with thousands of megaton weapons, each of which has a greater destructive power than all conventional explosives used since gunpowder was invented. Smaller nations rush to join the nuclear club. In 1973 the nations of the world spent $240 billion to train, equip, and maintain their armies—more than the total annual income of the poorest half of humankind. Allegedly to maintian a balance of power (and therefore "peace") but also certainly to preserve our affluent economy and our balance of payments, the U.S. and Canada have become major arms merchants in the sales of tanks, supersonic fighters, and missiles. The U.S. is now even selling nuclear reactors—to both sides in the Middle East. The outcome can only be tragedy.

Perhaps realism and rational self-interest will prevail, and Moscow, Washington, and Peking will manage to cling to détente. But that will not be peace. We hardly need the kind of unjust détente that the powerful rulers in the Kremlin and the Pentagon would ensure if they could.

I

What the world needs is not peace but revolution—not violent revolution but fundamental change in economic relationships between the poor and the rich. According to the most conservative U.N. estimates, at least 460 million people are permanently hungry.[2] A major cause of world hunger, of course, is unequal distribution, both within nations and among nations. The statistics are painfully familiar. Each American uses five times as much of the world's food resources each year as the average person in India. Although Americans have only 5 or 6 percent of the world's people, we consume 33 percent of its resources. Both directly through trade and economic policies and indirectly through support of unjust governments, Americans contribute to starvation.

As Jacques Ellul has insisted, unjust economic systems can be as violent as rampaging armies.

> I maintain that all kinds of violence are the same . . . the violence of the soldier who kills, the revolutionary who assassinates; it is true also of economic violence—the violence of the privileged proprietor against his workers, of the "haves" against the "have-nots"; the violence done in

international economic relations between our societies and those of the third world; the violence done through powerful corporations, which exploit the resources of a country that is unable to defend itself.[3]

And James Douglas concludes:

> In the contemporary world of affluence and poverty, where man's major crime is murder by privilege, revolution against the established order is the criterion of a living faith. ... Truly I say to you, as you did it not to one of the least of these, you did it not to me (Matthew 25:45). The murder of Christ continues. Great societies build on dying men.[4]

If Western Christians observe how our unjust economic structures produce suffering and starvation, they cannot fail to hear a divine summons to revolution. But it must be nonviolent revolution. Both pragmatic and theological considerations force one to that conclusion. Ellul among others has argued—convincingly, I think—that violence inevitably provokes more violence.

Nonviolent revolution is hardly a new vision. I would plead rather for a movement of *evangelical* nonviolence. I am persuaded that nothing short of a thoroughly biblical faith can provide the theoretical base and the staying power necessary to endure the discouragements and the agony of the impending struggle for justice.

A movement of evangelical nonviolence would immerse its direct action in prayer. Like Jesus, who agonized in prayer before facing the political and religious establishment of His day, it would pray for days and weeks for the transforming presence of the Holy Spirit before initiating a nonviolent campaign. It would make an evangelistic call for biblical repentance central to its approach. It would call upon politicians and business people to repent of their involvement in the institutionalized sin of economic justice. Finally, as a last resort, it would picket, boycott, obstruct, and paralyze unjust political and economic structures.

I am aware that most American evangelicals have been less than enthusiastic about pacifism. But in 1974 at the second national workshop of Evangelicals for Social Action, one proposal that was endorsed as a valid way to implement the Chicago Declaration of Evangelical Social Concern called for a movement of evangelical, nonviolent direct action. I am convinced that an evangelical commitment to biblical authority leads finally to nonviolence.

II

It is my contention that a biblical understanding of the cross leads necessarily to a nonviolent stance and, conversely, that only a fully biblical view of the cross and justification can provide an adequate foundation for nonviolence. As Dale Brown suggests, the "tendency to separate God's love of His enemies from our love of [our] enemies is one of the heresies of the doctrine of the atonement.[5]

The Sermon on the Mount calls us to turn the other cheek and love our enemies in imitation of the heavenly Father who bestows the gifts of nature on friend and foe alike (Matthew 5:43-48). The most vivid expression of divine love for enemies is the crucified Jesus praying for His executioners, "Father, forgive them, for they know not what they do." In Romans 5, Paul indicates that we perceive the depth of divine love only when we see that the crucified Jesus died for His enemies. "But God shows his love for us in that while we were yet sinners Christ died for us. ... While we were enemies we were reconciled to God by the death of his Son" (Romans 5:8-10). Love for enemies is at the heart of Jesus' work of atonement.

As John Howard Yoder has pointed out, the New Testament repeatedly calls on Christians to imitate the way of suffering love revealed in the cross.

> There is thus but one realm in which the concept of imitation [of Jesus] holds—but there it holds in every strand of the New Testament literature. ... This is at the point of the concrete social meaning of the cross in its relation to enmity and power. Servanthood replaces dominion, forgiveness absorbs hostility.[6]

In 1 Peter 2, Christian slaves of unjust masters are urged to imitate the way of the cross. "For to this you have been called, because Christ also suffered for you, leaving you an example, that you should follow in his steps. ... When he was reviled, he did not revile in return; when he suffered, he did not threaten" (1 Peter 2:21-23). "Be imitators of God," Ephesians 5 says, "and walk in love, as Christ loved us and gave himself up for us, a fragrant offering and sacrifice to God" (Ephesians 5:1, 2). The New Testament explicitly and repeatedly commands Christians to love their enemies in the nonviolent, self-sacrificing fashion of the crucified Jesus.

If evangelicals really believe that Jesus is Lord and that canonical Scripture is binding, then surely there is only one possibility. If Scripture calls us to love our enemies as Jesus loved His enemies at the cross, we must either accept the way of nonviolence or abandon our affirmation of scriptural authority. Since Jesus atoned for our sins by carrying love for enemy to the ultimate degree, a refusal to follow His example *at this point* not only involves a denial of scriptural authority; it also constitutes a questionable doctrine of the atonement. God chose to reconcile His enemies and accomplish the atonement by nonviolent, suffering love. If we reject the biblical imperative to follow Jesus at this point, we in effect express disbelief about the validity of God's way of reconciling enemies. But to do that is to express disbelief about the atonement itself.

Another heresy of the atonement also relates to our topic of nonviolence: some pacifists seem inclined to reduce the doctrine of the atonement to a revelation of God's method of dealing with evil. According to one writer in a collection of essays edited by the Quaker pacifist Rufus H. Jones, the cross is "Christ's witness to the weakness and folly of the sword.... Jesus is acknowledged as the Saviour precisely because He challenged and overthrew man's reliance upon military power."[7]

Certainly, as Leon Morris noted recently in *Christianity Today,* "no theory [of the atonement] is adequate. ... We need contributions of quite a few theories to express something of what the Cross meant to the men of the New Testament."[8] But to reduce the meaning of the cross either to a revelation of the validity of pacifism or to a powerful disclosure that God is love is simply unbiblical.

Whether or not modern theologians like it, the New Testament asserts not only that sinful persons are hostile to God but with equal clarity that the just Creator hates sin. Paul reminded the Romans that "the wrath of God is revealed from heaven against all ungodliness and wick-

edness" (Romans 1:18). For those who know the law,
failure to obey it results in a curse. But Christ redeemed
us from that curse by becoming a curse for us (Galatians
3:10-14). Jesus' blood is an expiation (Romans 5:18) for
sinners precisely because the One who knew no sin was
made sin for us on the cross (2 Corinthians 5:21). A pacifism which belittles or ignores this aspect of the cross
will not, for very sound reaons, find a welcome hearing
among evangelical Christians.

This understanding of the atonement relates to biblical
nonviolence in several ways. If it is true (a) that all
people are sinners and (b) that sin is not just an annoying
inconvenience to one's neighbors but also a damnable
outrage against our just God and (c) that God "desires all
men to be saved" (1 Timothy 2:4), then surely to kill
anyone who is not a Christian is to rob that person of the
opportunity to accept Christ as Savior. Moreover, although the way of violence dehumanizes and finally
destroys the oppressor, nonviolent resistance affirms the
oppressor's humanity and calls him to decision. Nonviolent resistance can be combined with an evangelistic call
to repentance. Because one challenges the oppressor with
a gentle firmness that underlines God's love even for
him, the evangelical practitioner of nonviolence can
invite the oppressor to repent and change even while opposing his evil actions.

III

I would also contend that only a biblical understanding that Jesus of Nazareth is now the risen Lord provides
an adequate authority and an unshakable hope for a nonviolent movement.

Most Christians agree that Jesus' approach to violent

persons was to suffer rather than to inflict suffering, to endure the cross rather than to use the dagger. His words are clear.

> You have heard that it was said, "An eye for an eye and a tooth for a tooth." But I say to you, Do not resist one who is evil. But if any one strikes you on the right cheek, turn to him the other also. . . . I say to you, Love your enemies and pray for those who persecute you (Matthew 5:38-44).

But Christians find ways to avoid the implications of such passages. Dispensationalists say that the Sermon on the Mount is meant only for the millennium; Lutherans argue that it applies only in personal relationships; Niebuhrians place it on a pedestal of irrelevance by honoring it as an impossible ideal.

Most evangelicals probably agree with Reinhold Niebuhr that in a world infested with well-armed Hitlers, Stalins, and colonialists, persons and nations that follow the way of the cross get wiped out. So one must sadly and repentantly fight wars for the sake of peace.

One way to respond to this argument is to return to the New Testament concept of what Jesus' resurrection implied. When Jesus came preaching the good news of the kingdom of heaven, He naturally aroused the messianic hope that the new age of peace and justice was at hand, when the dead would be resurrected and the Spirit poured out. He went about Palestine announcing that the kingdom of heaven was at hand, already beginning wherever people became His followers, forsook the values of Satan's kingdom, and started living the values of a very different kingdom. The early church also believed and taught that the new age had begun. Jesus' resurrection and the gift of the Spirit (Romans 8:23; Hebrews 6:5, 6) were seen as its first fruits. For the early church, Jesus' resurrection was tangible evidence that the new age had invaded the old eon. They knew, of course, that the kingdom would come in its fullness only at Christ's return when He would dethrone the principalities and powers and destroy death itself (1 Corinthians 15:20-24). But the resurrection was a visible sign that it made sense to begin living according to the standards of the new age which had proleptically invaded the old age.

The lifestyle of Christians ought to demonstrate their belief that the new age has begun. Christians do not claim that we should wait to live by the kingdom's standards on lying, theft, or adultery until non-Christians stop lying, stealing, and fornicating. Nor should the church delay implementing Jesus' nonviolent method of overcoming evil with good until the Caesars and Hitlers disappear.

The resurrection stands as God's tangible sign that implementing Jesus' nonviolent ethics now is not a foolish indication of a visionary fanatic but rather a sane submission to the One who is Lord of heaven and earth. That the resurrection was the decisive clue to Jesus' identity is clear in every strand of early Christian literature. Before the resurrection, the disciples called Him Master and rabbi; afterward they said, "My Lord and my God." From Acts it is clear that it was the resurrection that led the disciples to confess Jesus as Lord (Acts 2:32-36; 5:30, 31).

In Philippians 2, Paul writes, "God has highly exalted him and bestowed on him the name which is above every name, that at the name of Jesus every knee should bow, in heaven and on earth and under the earth, and every tongue confess that Jesus Christ is Lord" (Philippians 2:9-11; cf. Isaiah 45:23). By applying these words to Jesus, Paul fills the confession "Jesus Christ is Lord" with the most lofty meaning imaginable. If that is who Jesus of Nazareth is, then surely one simply obeys. If the One who called His followers to love their enemies is the Lord of the universe, then surely any attempt to circumvent or ignore His teaching should be unthinkable.

IV

Jesus' resurrection anchors our hope. That nonviolent movements often disintegrate in despair when they experience the full force of organized injustice and systemic evil is clear. A new movement of evangelical nonviolence must anticipate the same temptation. We will not begin with an unbiblical view of progress or a humanistic view of the goodness of persons. We do not naively expect that a winning smile and a short homily will tame the Hitlers and the white supremacists of this age. This will be suffering. But our commitment is steadied by the certainty that our Lord Jesus experienced all the evil and agony that the fallen principalities and powers could inflict, and nevertheless He conquered them in his resurrection.

If the One who advocated nonviolent love and suffering as the true way to overcome our enemies had been destroyed by evil at the cross, if He had remainded in death, then we would have to conclude that death and failure are the final word for those who live nonviolently. But He is risen! The resurrection stands as a powerful sign that the nonviolent way will ultimately prevail.

The exultant New Testament view that Jesus triumphed over the principalities and powers in the resurrection offers a sure foundation for enduring hope. In Ephesians 1, we read that God "raised him [Jesus] from the dead and made him sit at his right hand in the heavenly places, far above all rule and authority and power and dominion, and above every name that is named ... he has put all things under his feet" (Ephesians 1:20-22). It is clear in 1 Corinthians 15 that because of Jesus' resurrection Paul could declare confidently that the risen Lord will, at His coming, complete the victory over every rule and authority and power (1 Corinthians 15:24).

Because of Jesus' resurrection and the resulting assurance of our Lord's final victory, it is a mistake to relate effectiveness and faithfulness in terms of either/or. Sometimes, in the short run, it may seem that they are incompatible and that we must choose one or the other. But the resurrection is our Lord's reminder that His followers must not be misled by the short-term view. Even in terms of relatively short periods of time, of course, nonviolence has often proved amazingly effective. But the resurrection assures us that in the long run the way of the nonviolent cross is also the way of the resurrected Sovereign of the universe.

Precisely at this point, a question forces itself upon us. Will *any* understanding of the resurrection be an adequate foundation for our hope? In his powerful book *The Non-Violent Cross* James Douglas makes a great deal of the resurrection, but for him the resurrection is only a symbol of oppressed people's awakening to the power of nonviolence. "Man becomes God when Love and Truth enter into man, not by man's power but by raising him to Power, so that revolution in love is revealed finally as the Power of resurrection."[9]

Such a view is both unbiblical and inadequate. If by Jesus' resurrection we mean merely the birth of nonviolent convictions or the inner assurance of the early Christians that they should continue to follow the way of the Nazarene, then our hope is based on nothing more than our own subjectivity. As Paul argued in 1 Corinthians 15, if Jesus of Nazareth had not been raised from the tomb, then Christian faith is useless.

The fact of the resurrection assures us that the way of nonviolent love will ultimately prevail. Our nonviolent campaign can be joyful celebrations of His coming victory at the same time that we experience the cross of police brutality, prison, and death. We know that the kingdoms of the world shall become the kingdom of our Lord and the nonviolent One shall reign forever.

V

Finally, one pressing objection remains. Is not an appeal for an activist movement of direct albeit nonviolent confrontation with evil social structures fundamentally incompatible with Jesus' call for nonresistance? Did not Jesus urge us to turn the other cheek rather than picket, to refuse to "resist one who is evil" rather than boycott unjust companies? And surely a call for evangelical nonviolence contradicts Paul's command in Romans 13 to submit to the powers that be!

It seems to me that Jesus' own actions show that a quietist interpretation of His command not to resist one who is evil (Matthew 5:39) is mistaken. Jesus' cleansing of the temple provides the clearest evidence. Jesus engaged in aggressive resistance against evil when He marched into the temple, drove the animals out with a whip, overturned the money tables of the businessmen and denounced their defiling of the temple. If Matthew 5 means that all forms of resistance are forbidden, then Jesus contradicted His own teaching. Jesus certainly did not kill and probably did not whip the money changers, but He did resist their evil in an act of civil disobedience.

Nor was Jesus passive in His vigorous attack on the Pharisees. Denouncing them as blind guides, fools, hypocrites, and a brood of vipers, He uttered harsh public words condemning them for their preoccupation with small matters and their neglect of more important things such as justice and mercy (Matthew 23).

In John 18:19-24, we see how Jesus responded to the soldier who unjustly struck Him on the cheek. The text does not say that Jesus submitted meekly to this injustice. He protested! Jesus replied, "If I have spoken wrongly, bear witness to the wrong; but if I have spoken rightly, why do you strike me?" That Jesus respected the authorities at His trial is clear. But apparently His way of nonviolent love was not at all incompatible with protesting police brutality or engaging in civil disobedience in a nonviolent fashion. When we interpret Matthew 5:39 in the light of Jesus' own perfect example and actions in confronting evil persons, we see that the quietist interpretation is a distortion.

Nor do I think the widespread quietistic interpretation of Romans 13 among evangelicals is valid. Historically, a solid Reformed tradition has explicitly argued that Romans 13 does not preclude resistance against unjust rulers. No less a person than John Knox argued that when rulers act unjustly and fail to punish sin and protect virtue, they lose their divine authority and must be resisted and overthrown. Let us grant that since govern-

ment is ordained of God, all governments—even very
unjust ones—possess a significant degree of authority although God hates their injustices and will eventually
destroy them. Even bad governments can prevent chaos
and preserve order. Hence the Christian respects and
submits to their authority.

But only to a point. When Paul tells us to give honor
where honor is due, one hears echoes of Jesus' advice to
give to Caesar what is Caesar's and to God what is God's.
And Paul and the early church regularly defied the
government when it demanded that they abandon their
loyalty to Jesus and His kingdom. Because Christians
owe absolute loyalty only to the kingdom, we dare offer
only very limited, conditional loyalty to governments.
Whenever governments call on us to act contrary to the
demands and values of the kingdom, we must respectfully decline.

VI

Evangelicals have regularly approved and applied this
principle of conditional obedience in the case of preaching and personal ethics. If governments forbid public
worship or preaching, or command lying or adultery, it
is, as Peter said, better to obey God than man. But evangelicals have not extended this principle to social ethics.
Is there any way to justify this selective application?

I think not. Perhaps if one made the unbiblical
assumption that evangelism is primary and social action
is secondary,[10] one could argue that one should resist the
governing authorities in order to preach the gospel but
not to work for social justice. Perhaps if one adopted the
recent evangelical heresy that orthodoxy is more important than orthopraxis, one might be able to argue the

case. But surely those who emphasize right doctrine
more than faithful practice ignore both a major part of
the evangelical tradition and the Bible. One of the major
concerns of John Wesley in the Evangelical Awakening
was to correct an empty creedalism largely unconcerned
with living the Christian life. First John says bluntly that
any claim to know and love God which is divorced from
loving the hungry neighbor is a hypocritical lie (1 John
3:15-18; 4:7-12).

The converse, of course, is also true. Orthodoxy is as
important as orthopraxis. I John, which emphasizes the
importance of concrete love for neighbor, also insists that
he who does not confess that Jesus the Messiah is the incarnate Son of God is the Antichrist (1 John 2:22-25; 4:1-
3, 15, 16).

Loyalty to the kingdom then may compel one to resist
governments for the sake of both evangelistic proclamation and social justice. Of course, Christians will continue
to respect even the most unjust governments as they
develop nonviolent campaigns to witness to injustice and
press for radical change. They will at times refuse to
cooperate with unjust structures, but they will not try to
avoid the consequent penalties.

One major focus of such a movement should be an attempt to change the exploitive economic relationship
between the rich and the poor nations. As Jacques Ellul
argues, "Unless Christians fulfill their prophetic role, unless they become the advocates and defenders of the
truly poor ... then infallibly violence will suddenly
break out."[11] The present food crisis is the tip of the iceberg of economic exploitation. Unless the West can
somehow be persuaded to reduce drastically its affluent
life style and thereby to lessen its economic exploitation

of the poor countries, it is unlikely that wars can be avoided. For example, when tens of millions of Indians begin starving, India's government will be sorely tempted to try nuclear blackmail. And we will fight to defend our affluence.

I dream of a movement of evangelical, nonviolent, direct action that will dare to pray and picket, evangelize and blockade, until Americans can no longer ignore the way our affluence is built on poverty and starvation abroad. I dream of a movement that will agonize in prayer for weeks as Jesus did in the garden before beginning a direct-action campaign against multinational corporations engaged in injustice abroad. I dream of biblical Christians who will initiate the campaign with a loving call to repentance from the sin of economic injustice. We will believe that God may even choose to convert those who head unjust multinational corporations. But we dare not stop with verbal communication. Civil disobedience infused with prayer, evangelistic proclamation, and a profound respect for law and government will be necessary. I dream of a movement of biblical Christians who even as they are carted off to jail will express Christ-like tenderness to policemen, who even as they are sentenced will explain Jesus' way of love and justice to incredulous judges, who will even dare to risk their own lives in order to release the captives and free the oppressed. By word and sign we must witness to the principalities and powers in the affluent countries that unjust economic structures are an abomination to the Lord of the universe. Only a movement of evangelical nonviolence is adequate for that task.[12]

5

THE CONTEMPORARY EVANGELICAL REVIVAL AND THE PEACE CHURCHES

John H. Yoder

I shall attempt to describe, or perhaps even to a degree to prescribe, the relationship between two distinct phenomena, each of them described with a rather broad and a general label. I shall need, of course, to fill in what I understand to be important about the definition of each of those phenomena identified in the title, before moving on to suggest what their relationships are or could be.

This description and prescription will be approached in three ways. First, I shall seek to determine what is meant by the phrase "contemporary evangelical revival," and to analyze the questions which arise when one attempts to relate to that from a denominationally defined perspective. In other words, I shall identify the problems which arise when one assumes that "evangelicalism" and "the peace churches" are quite independent quantities, both of which exist separately and with clear definition, before we try to relate them to one another. Second, I shall suggest another way of responding to the same question without making the polarized presuppositions which seem to first underline the way the title was phrased.[1]

Third, and at more length because it raises questions of substance and not only form, I shall try to describe with more care the content of an evangelical peace witness as that relates to two specific challenges of modern American evangelical identity: Whether a major controverted ethical issue like the war question can be dealt with in evangelical polity, and how to understand the classical but confusing traditional distinction between nonessentials and essentials.

I

First, there is the identity problem. One way of putting the question is to assume that the peace churches are known as a body with clear identity, within which we are now assumed to be speaking, and that "the contemporary evangelical revival" is a much larger and equally evident phenomenon "out there." In other words, the question itself as it is phrased presupposes certain assumptions and certain questions about denominational identity. It presupposes that peace churches are a group different from the phenomenon out there. For example, although Mennonites have an identity, they probably also have doubts about that identity. They once had an identity clearly distinguishable from anything out there, but now they need to relate to the rest of the world, including the rest of the Christian world. It is easier to do that if we can find a specific thrust in that Christian

world out there to which we can relate. We may find
something out there that we can identify as a good thing
to join, and thus feel better about the erosion of our
identity, or we may locate a bad thing to keep away from
and feel less ashamed of our separateness. For many
Mennonites the "evangelical movement" represents a
clear, self-confident, and respectable external identity on
which to focus. This then becomes a way to deal with the
challenge of acculturation. This is the challenge which
the wider world—this time the wider Christian world—
addresses to who they are. Peace churches ascribe to
evangelicalism the qualities they sense to be lacking in
their own family—clear answers, effectiveness, and self-
confidence.

The word "evangelical" has had many meanings down
through history. Its root meaning is simply that which is
derived from the gospel, from the evangel. But, of
course, when any term is used to 'describe a phenomenon, a movement, a person, a thought, as distinct from
other phenomena or movements, it means something
more precise than its linguistic root meaning. The oldest
meaning which still influences our society is "non-
Catholic." It means "stemming from the Reformation."
The major national churches of German-speaking
Europe today are called Evangelical Lutheran or Evangelical Reformed, meaning that they are not Catholic
churches. In the Catholic parts of the world today all
non-Catholics—Lutheran, Reformed, even Anglical, to
say nothing of Baptist, Mennonite, and Pentecostal—are
lumped together as evangelicals.

The next oldest meaning comes from a particular
development in the history of the Church of England at
the beginning of the nineteenth century. That com-

munion is an inclusive church. Its philosophy is that every believing Englishman ought to be able to be a member. It has room for different strands and tendencies within its membership, and different groupings are encouraged to form within the larger "church." The modern term for this phenomenon is "caucus," a group of people within a larger group who get together in order to have a common impact. In the Church of England there was an Anglo-Catholic caucus or fraction which accentuated the liturgy, especially the eucharist, and the importance of bishops, and expressed a desire for reunion with the church of Rome. There was an "evangelical" fraction which accentuated the importance of personal experience, the proclamation of the faith to unbelievers, the study of the Bible, a vital prayer life, and such matters. They stayed within the Church of England and within that church formed their own seminary, retreat centers, information network, and publications. This was neither divisive nor improper since this is the proper way to deal with diversity in the Church of England. In order to organize a caucus, you accentuate what you hold that differentiates you from others, presupposing what you have in common with others. Thus, evangelical Anglicans continue to believe in bishops, subscribe to the Thirty-nine Articles, baptize infants, and go to war at the call of the queen or king. The identity of the caucus accentuates what you agree upon, but you agree on many things with the wider group as well.

Moving to North America, in the course of the nineteenth century, a new social form for the Christian church was created in the Midwest and part of the South. Here the churches were all of the free church pattern. Although some had synods or conferences, and some had bishops, a congregationally ordered kind of church became the standard form, the "establishment," in Middle America. Preaching called for personal decision. Most churches called for experiences of renewal as persons grew in faith. Thus in Middle America we had "established religion" in the social sense, a religion which dominated the social order, but whose form was that of the free churches and whose message was a simple biblical call to conversion or sanctification, or to personal experience in growing depth, expressed by that event called the revival. Revival, the camp meeting, replaces the bishop as the way to hold the church together.

This new Christian culture has often been referred to as the "Bible Belt." This society is psychologically conservative because it is an established order. Most of the respectable and powerful people attend these churches. These are the people who have an investment in the shape of things as they are, in patriotism, in the American experience of freedom, and the economic system called free enterprise. This society is conservative intellectually. Its members associate the authority of the Bible with other things which they believe. They are opposed to changes in intellectual mood. When Darwin comes along they oppose evolution. When Marx comes along they oppose social changes in the direction of greater sharing. When Freud comes along they are against looking inside the personality to see what makes it tick. All of this resistance to change is done in the name of an established culture which appeals to the Bible for its authority. Although this position was not *at first* called "evangelical," it has been an important part of our cultural experience.

Finally, we need to look at a coalition in our history. A

coalition differs from a caucus. A coalition is formed by those who unite around something which they have in common *against* other forces on the wider scene. That wider scene is not seen to be a unity like the Church of England. Adversaries are not recognized as representing legitimate alternatives within the same church. In order to form a coalition, members identify those things which they hold in common as "essentials" and those things on which they properly may differ as "nonessentials."

The coalition under consideration here is that which began in the first part of the century under the name "fundamentalism." The essentials were the "fundamentals," items of belief that it was considered impossible to differ on and still work together. Off to the side there were other matters, "nonessentials," on which one could differ and still work together. A coalition always had an adversary. The adversary of fundamentalism was "modernism," a mood and development within the American churches which represented change away from the older traditions, especially those which the "fundamentals" identified. Differing lists of "the fundamentals" were produced by different groups, but they always had something to do with the authority of the Bible, with the meaning of the atonement, and with personal change or being born again. The things that did not matter were the things that Christians had differed on before. Some of our forefathers were put to death for thinking that infant baptism made a difference. Now it was a nonessential. So were going to war or not, the issue of free will, or differences about the reality or the completeness of sanctification. What was important was agreement on the things considered strategic for this particular battle against modernism.

Who joined this coalition? It brought together people
of very different backgrounds for whom these fundamental statements had different meanings. It included
people from the Bible Belt establishment for whom the
major church form would be Southern Baptist. It included small churches with no history, independent Bible churches, groups gathered together by gifts of a
certain preacher, and young small denominations. It included some members of cultural enclave churches who
had gone less far into Americanization such as the
Missouri Synod Lutherans and the Christian Reformed
people who had a very solid rooting in another history.
They had never changed on such questions as biblical authority and felt close to the battle against the modernists
although they were not satisfied with the theologies
involved. Some Mennonites found themselves in this
same circle. Some individuals and congregations within
the mainline denominations held similar views. That
coalition was a very important part of American church
experience from the First until the Second World War.

After the Second World War the coalition had new
troubles. Some elements became more narrow and com-
bative, others more educated, inclusive, and polite. The
word "fundamentalist" had, in some circles, taken on a
flavor that was distasteful. It came to represent more nar-
rowness and rigidity than some wanted to be associated
with. For that reason the word "evangelical" was
adopted in the early postwar period. It became a label for
the coalition which permitted it to leave behind some of
the less tasteful expressions of combativeness and rigidity
while still holding to the same fundamental witness. The
term evangelical was chosen partly because of the continuing conversations with Anglo-Saxon churches around

the world, particularly in Britain, where the word "evangelical" had the "caucus" meaning described above, a legitimate fraction within the Church of England with links to other churches in England. The use of the word "evangelical" itself was part of the strategy of coalition, using words to bring a group together. This was dramatized by the creation of the National Association of Evangelicals in which some Mennonites and Brethren in Christ were formally represented from the beginning. From then until the present, this institutionalized evangelicalism has grown in the quality and institutional power of its expression in our society.

What then are the issues in relationships and cooperation between peace churches and Evangelicals today? If events would stand still, it would be possible simply to itemize similarities and differences, asking what the Christian pattern should be for taking seriously both what enables us to recognize one another as fellow Christians doing together what we can and, at the same time, to remain honest about real differences such as nationalism, pedobaptism, and war. As I wrote twenty years ago,[2] this should call for more cooperation and for less ethnic and institutional self-sufficiency than Mennonites regularly practice, as well as for more clarity and accountability about significant distinctives. Combining cooperativeness and distinctiveness is not a simple matter, but it is possible and many of our church leaders in missions, relief, publications, and education have been doing so with some care for years.

However, the task still includes major problems, especially:

(a) The relationship between outreach agencies which have been cooperative for a long time and local congregational experience where there has been less working together, and

(b) The relationship of the peace witness to other "distinctives" which we have traditionally called "nonconformity" or "simplicity." Many have considered the "distinctives" all of one piece, so that those who are at home in the counterculture of buggies, cape dresses, and no neckties doubt that the peace witness can be shared with "worldly Christians." Those who want to show themselves liberated from that ethnic culture tend to think that the peace witness is part of what has been outgrown or become embarrassed about. The history of the impact of varied meanings of "separation" upon our ability to witness and to cooperate has yet to be clarified.

The challenge is also complex because evangelicalism itself is changing. The simplicity of the evangelical consensus has been shaken up. The clarity of what that movement is has been jeopardized by events and changes in the last decade.

One such event is called the "charismatic renewal." It logically belongs within the coalition. It is biblical. It talks about the power of the Spirit to change people; it is evangelistic. But there is no consensus about whether or not it belongs in the movement. Certain groups in the evangelical coalition do not approve of this new kind of experience. Divisions on this issue exist within the churches, evangelical schools, conferences, and organizations. A further complication is that this charismatic renewal has also found its way within Roman Catholicism. Evangelical, we remember, used to mean non-Catholic. Although anti-Catholicism was not stated as one of the five fundamentals, it was taken for granted that anyone who believes in the Bible and believes in

tion in a new "battle around the Bible" which must affect the self-confidence of the movement.

Finally, other hopes have collapsed. There was a time, not too long ago, when liberal humanism was impressive. Some thought that civil rights action would change the world. Some thought that Vietnam protests would change our culture and turn the nation around. Others had other causes. Most of these causes have collapsed. Now there is a new respect for some of the older patterns, not because these older patterns have proven themselves more effective, but simply because with their deeper cultural roots they are still around when other visions have faded.

With this much description, it is apparent that if we thought that the contemporary evangelical revival was a well-defined train that we had only to look at to decide whether to get on or not (or perhaps to add a peace church caboose), it does not have that kind of solidity. Furthermore, the attempt to clarify one's identity problem by latching on to something else which is more confident is not a very wholesome kind of psychology. Therefore my effort to answer our question by assuming that the evangelical revival is one clear entity and that the peace churches are another and then asking what our relationship might be has not led us firmly anywhere.

II

Let me then try to come at the question in another way. This way may seem presumptuous or to be playing with words. This way is to claim that the peace church vision is itself the logically consistent form of evangelical revival. Thus the question is not one of tagging along behind someone else's evangelicalism. Rather, the gospel points (among other things) to a peace message. Thus, pardon the slang way of expressing this, the peace churches are the train and non-peace caucuses, "evangelicals" who duck the war issue, are the caboose. Historically, this was the case. Each of the peace church movements arose as an evangelical revival which broke through certain barriers into the creation of a new style. Whether it be the youngest, the Brethren and the River Brethren, whether it be George Fox, the sixteenth-century Anabaptists, or the fifteenth-century Czech Brethren, in each case the message which we now call evangelical reached beyond superficial renewal and created a new community of spirit, conversion, outreach, and biblical authority. All of the peace churches come from such origins. Each peace church represents an evangelical renewal which went all the way into renewal of church order and social style.

Put conversely, each of the elements of evangelical identity itself calls for a Christian peace-making witness. Peace-making is in chapter five of Matthew. It is not as passive as the interpretation of "nonresistance" has often been. If this is the clear implication of the evangelical message, how is it to be spelled out concretely? Ronald Sider's paper in this volume spells out many of these implications. I seek here to say some of the same things in other words. If one looks clearly at the moral and spiritual value of what evangelicalism claims to be saying, one cannot explain not being a pacifist.

What does evangelicalism say? It speaks of power for change, of vital personal faith. It speaks out of a focus on the Spirit, of resurrection, of the coming new age or the present new age, of conversion or the radicality of new birth. The language may change, but any evangelical message must speak of power for change. According to Jesus and the common Christian heritage, this is the basis for a new lifestyle.

Second, any movement that calls itself evangelical must talk about Scripture as authority for change. This authority is a slightly, but significantly different way of understanding the power of Scripture than is found in some other "evangelical" contexts. In some high church contexts the debate is about holding to a confession of faith or to a systematic theological statement or to a book such as the Lutheran Book of Concord. The system of thought has authority because it is believed to be based on the Bible. In another kind of Protestantism the debate is about the status of the text. We have this Book whose words were given by God in a specific event for which we have the technical term "inspiration." Then we debate the status of the text. Although this debate is better than the one that went before, it is not what the Anabaptists debated. Nor is it what the early Puritans and George Fox and Alexander Mack debated. They were not bothered about where the text came from. Their debate was about whether it was to be obeyed, about whether the text is for us, whether it is a power for change and will keep driving for change, about whether it enables criticism of conformity, rejection of consensus, and provides the shape of an alternative consciousness and a basis for ongoing renewal.

Some in the peace churches may have thought that a radical reformation occurs once and then they are only called upon to conserve that radical heritage which they have from the fathers. But if we really believe that Scripture is a power for change we must come out at a different point. We come out with the expectation of ongoing growth. The preacher who said good-bye to the radical Puritans who left Plymouth for New England, John Robinson, made a statement in his farewell sermon that has been widely quoted. "The Lord has yet more truth to break forth from his Holy Word." We should not merely be grateful for the clarity attained about something we have already learned, but rather should expect more cultural criticism, more depth of discovery, if we keep on living with the Scriptures. This insight is not the same as fine-tuned debates about the phrasing of statements about inspiration and inerrancy. This is the way that the Bible wants to be taken—as power for change. If one takes it this way, there is no room for war.

Third, evangelicalism has to do with the normativeness of Jesus. Sometimes discussions center on whether what matters most about Jesus is His ethical teachings such as those in Matthew 5—7, or the believers' personal experience of Him as we have it described in the Epistles. I not only refuse to choose between these two, but insist that more important than both of these is the Person of Jesus Himself, a Man who lived, had a social career, got Himself crucified, and rose from the dead. You cannot make Him central and go to war.

Evangelicalism has always meant world mission. You cannot think of the world as needing to be won for Christian faith and think of any nation as an enemy to be destroyed. You cannot think of your message as power to win people of other cultures and social systems, people who pledge allegiance to other civil sovereignties, and still tolerate your nation's treatment of them as enemies.

For a long time Christians, including many in the evangelical movement, have not seen this problem. Now, in conversations with the younger churches in the younger nations, we are seeing much more clearly the extent to which North American and European patriotic religion has made the gospel a scandal in other parts of the world. A true understanding of the missionary impact of the evangelical identity excludes war and violence.

Another part of the evangelical identity has been the creation of a body of believers. Although the message from the pulpit often sounded individualistic, as it focused on the heart of the individual believer, the impact of the message was always to create community, groups of people who no longer took their signals from the wider society, who developed their own social style, sometimes their own culture, and occasionally even their own language. The gospel enables believers to live against the stream of the wider society. The Christian peace witness cannot be the position only of a few heroic conscientious objectors or a few prophetic figures who say what is wrong with war. It must be the lived witness of a counter community.

Other things could be listed. There is the personalizing impact of evangelical faith which leads us to think of both the oppressor and the victims of oppression as persons rather than only as elements in political systems or as statistics. There is the vision of the cross which tells us that sacrifice and failure may be meaningful, usable in God's purposes, in the face of our age's appetite for effectiveness. There is the trust in providence and the coming kingdom which enables us to renounce the temptation to make history come out right by means of violence. This trust may not mean that discussing practicality is irrelevant, but it does mean that effectiveness is not the first or last word in weighing what we are to do about conflict. Within the evangelical movement there has always been the readiness to create the new social forms. The newly visible thrusts of "evangelicals for social action" in its liberal, radical, and moderate forms only looks new because we are shortsighted. Wesley did that. Finney did that. Every major renewal movement in the past has created social service institutions and has radiated into political life. Every spiritual renewal movement has had a new impact on the wider society. Whether that impact occurs automatically so that we need not talk of effectiveness or whether it needs to be thought about so that we must talk about effectiveness is a major subject in itself. The concerns here is that the expectation that the gospel will make a difference in the way a country runs has always been a part of the evangelical thrust.

These sample propositions should be sufficient to state the thesis that the wholesome way to understand the Historical Peace Church tradition is as the consistent outworking of evangelical renewal which God has repeatedly brought to the surface.

That which has called itself "the contemporary evangelical revival" is really less than that because it has yet to face the problems of nationalism, war, intercommunity violence, and personal lifestyle with full trust in the power of the gospel to make changes in all of these. If we can overcome our feelings of both inferiority at some points and superiority at others, and learn to reformulate the message of reconciliation in gospel terms, "the contemporary evangelical revival" might just be open to taking that step of trust tomorrow.

If that hope has real meaning, it will be useful to come at the question once more at greater depth. To restate the problem: The traditions of Mennonites since the early sixteenth century, Friends since the seventeenth, the Brethren since the early eighteenth, and Brethren in Christ since the late eighteenth, have in common the conviction that killing and military service are incompatible with the Christian calling. This is an issue of fundamental social significance. A position differing from that of society at large on such a matter is taken only at considerable emotional cost. Thus it is a position which, as long as it is held with any conviction at all, makes up a considerable portion of the self-understanding of the Historic Peace Churches.

On the other hand, at least a sizable portion of the membership of the Historic Peace Churches, and certainly for all of them in the age of their beginnings, the Christian faith has been conceived in terms which today are called "evangelical." Their biblical orientation, missionary concern, insistence upon genuineness in personal appropriation of faith, and concern for holiness of life find their closest parallels in the heritage of frontier evangelicalism.

The problem with which we are to deal here is the relationship between these two facts; on the one hand a distinctive conviction which, if held at all, must be taken quite seriously; and on the other a sense of community and a common rejection of official, conformist, politically respectable Christendom which gives a sense of kinship with the kind of "evangelicalism" represented in the National Association of Evangelicals.[3]

In order to understand this relationship we need a theological treatment of the biblical, historical, and systematic issues related to this peace testimony, a treatment which cannot even be sketched here. It is significant, however, that statements of the peace church position have not received serious brotherly attention from non-pacifist evangelicals. There has been little serious effort on the part of non-pacifist evangelicals to explain the compatibility of war with Christianity.

For the present we can only seek to speak of the nature of the conversational situation in which we find ourselves and of the challenge presented by this situation, as the peace churches find themselves widely represented in evangelical circles.

The present context is especially appropriate for conversations among evangelical Protestants around the issue of war and peace with regard to the nature of war, specifically *the just war theory and modern war.* Although not given to extensive theoretical argument, non-pacifist evangelicalism belongs basically within the framework of the traditional theology of the "just war." By this is meant the conviction that it is possible to distinguish between wars which are wrong and those which are permissible. If this distinction is to be taken seriously, and Christians refuse to give a total blank check to any and all governments, this must be done by weighing the destructiveness of the given war effort against the values which it seeks to defend.

The development of new weapons which are less controllable and immensely more destructive than in the Middle Ages when the just war theory was developed can change the conclusions without changing the basic logic. When more noncombatant civilians are involved, and when it is less self-evident that the desired values will be served by the military effort, this can lead persons who had been able to make a case for a traditional "ideal," "conventional" kind of war, when waged against tyranny for the sake of freedom, to become more critical and questioning. Not only do the atomic weapons already developed and used against Japan, and the new means of intercontinental delivery change war in a radical way; the concept of total war, the bacteriological and chemical weapons not yet used, or guerrilla warfare and counter-insurgency methods are similarly harder to justify morally. Perhaps the mass media reporting on the realities of the Vietnam war has also contributed to a greater degree of moral awareness as to the inhumane character even of subatomic weapons.

A second issue appropriate to further conversations concerns the *assumptions about the religious character of the American national identity*. The national self-understanding of the Protestant American, despite the formal separation of the church and the state as organizations, is clearly that America is a Protestant country and subject to a special divine vocation and protection. The nation's being Protestant, being righteous, being blessed by God, and winning all its wars have all fitted together into one spiritual unity. This picture has contributed more decisively to the formation of the American character and to the making of specific political decisions than has any detailed study of specific moral issues. We won all our wars because we were on the right side. That we were on the right side was true by definition because of the kind of nation we are; whether in any given conflict the position taken by our government was morally the right one did not need to be a subject of objective evaluation.

Now this picture has been undermined from several sides. The Protestant "establishment by consensus" has been eaten away by sociological and legal realism, recognizing the rights both of other religions and of nonreligious citizens. The identification of the church with the American cause has been further challenged by the perspective of Christian missionaries and by increasing theological self-awareness. In the postcolonial world Americans have learned slowly, with some dismay, that the rest of the world does not share this picture of America as source of all virtue, even when other nations are living on our food.

This vision of righteous America has been undermined most radically by the recognition that, without being fully aware of it, and without new legal action, our nation was involved in a colonial and civil war which even traditional allies could not understand or support, and which for the first time in our history was morally condemned by a significant portion of the nation's intellectual and religious leaders.

It was possible—although the peace churches would argue on biblical-evangelical grounds that it was wrong— to conceive of participation in the Second World War as clearly justified in view of the great evil represented by the Axis powers. Now even the persons who argue that the Vietnam war was justified cannot make of it that kind of crusade. Many more, even if they have not the readiness to choose the path of conscientious objection, are deeply aware that there is something wrong with America's moral self-consciousness.

This recognition does not mean that evangelicals are ready to reverse radically their understanding of this war or of all wars. It may mean a possible openness to look at a question which had previously been thought closed.

A third element of relative novelty within the "evangelical" camp which could lead to further discussion is a *growing theological perspective on the process of study and theological controversy.* For a long time, organized evangelicalism has operated under two assumptions which radically simplified the intellectual task. On the one hand, because of the basic Protestant claim that the Bible's message is perspicuous and understandable to the common man as far as essentials are concerned, it was not felt that much further study or debate was needed around any essential topics. Second, the agreement to accept diversity in "nonessentials" without making an issue of them provided a ready explanation for leaving untouched points at which there was difference.

The Congress on the Church's World Wide Mission[4] held at Wheaton in 1966 demonstrated a growing maturity on the part of evangelical Christian leaders, in the awareness that even after affirming a common submission to biblical authority, Christians need seriously to continue to study together issues concerning which different convictions are possible, that the very process of study itself must be given formal attention, and that means must be found for handling ideas in group process. There may, therefore, be some grounds for hope that there is a greater capacity for dealing with theological difference within a framework of mutual respect and acceptance than has sometimes in the past been typical of conservative theologies.

At the same time that these changes have occurred within evangelicalism, one also notes new resources for conversation within the peace church context. Based on conversations within the Mennonite churches, it seems clear that there is a deepening of our understanding of the peace position and the reasons for it, which should enable its more adequate communication.

The age has passed when peace church people could conceive of themselves as a cultural and ethnic minority, deriving their identity from their ancestors and a migration history. Both a sense of community with the wider Protestant world, and the conviction that the peace position is, rather than an ethnic peculiarity or privilege, a matter of simple Christian obedience has increased. As long as the rank and file of the church think of the peace position as a matter of particular folklore, even though they cherish it, they cannot communicate it. That time is rapidly passing.

Together with this development, and with the learning we have been privileged to do at the feet of the preachers of the American revival movements, there has come as well a *shift in our understanding of the nature of ethics.* As long as we were speaking only to ourselves, it was possible for our understanding of Christian ethics to focus upon less than fully adequate concepts. One such inadequate focus was a literalistic interpretation of the Sermon on the Mount or the Ten Commandments as simply forbidding war. This we could say without needing any deeper understanding of the why and the wherefore. Another such possible focus was upon the experience of regeneration, or sanctification, or nonconformity, whereby the logic of being called to be radically different from the surrounding world was itself taken as an adequate foundation.

The need to converse with other Christian groups, and the deepening biblical and theological studies of recent generations, have contributed to a heightened capacity to root the Christian peace witness more centrally in the authority and the character of Christ, not only as Teacher but also as the One perfectly obedient Man. The kind of understanding of the meaning of the cross to which I shall refer below has also been to a considerable extent for the peace churches a new discovery, or rather a rediscovery of the rootage which the Historic Peace Church attitude toward war originally had.

The peace witness has been given more positive expression in the development of service programs and other expressions of social concern both at home and abroad. It has thus moved from concentration upon a prohibition at the extreme point where government makes certain demands of a few young men, to a broader understanding of the posture of servanthood which should characterize the presence of the total body of Christ in the world.

It is possible, further, to discern the faint outline of a particular position, characteristic of the free church and peace church heritages, which refuses to be satisfied with the present polarization of the concern for Christian unity. Although feeling broadly at home within the mainstream of American evangelicalism, the peace churches are especially dismayed at the ease with which this movement or at least some of its spokesmen can fall into the temptations of provincialism and nationalism. As free churches with a relatively congregationalistic heritage we are not sure either about the confidence which organized evangelicalism places in doctrinal statements, nor about the particular promotional methods whereby interdenominational and nondenominational agencies compete in creating new institutional forms.

Although sensing a certain community of interest at the program level with churches of the American ecumenical mainstream, as concerns social needs and overseas relief, it continues to be difficult for the peace churches to feel at home in that context because of the theological varieties, the heavy bureaucracy, and the assumed posture of moral leadership in all of American society which tend to characterize these agencies.

In the past, this feeling of not belonging in either camp has driven peace church groups to retreat and not to participate actively in relations with other Christians on *either* "side"; or they have maintained a timid contact without feeling free to speak up except when spoken to.

Although this is a hazardous prediction, more than it is a descriptive statement, I would suggest that we can discern on the horizon a growing awareness that it is unnecessary to let one's position be dictated by the options provided by the situation, with the implication that it is possible to speak with somewhat more confidence from one's own footing. This experience of not fitting precisely in either camp, which in an earlier generation meant being embarrassed and on the margin of both, is now perhaps more likely to be seen as a specific calling.

III

After noting these changes both within evangelicalism and the peace churches one might also note evangelicalism changes in thought on matters of social ethics. Here we have to deal with what Carl Henry once called "the uneasy conscience of modern fundamentalism." We find in conservative evangelical circles a growing awareness that the realm of social ethics is one to which the Bible speaks and to which Christians cannot avoid speaking, even if they have in the past sought to avoid taking responsibility for what they said or to avoid considering what they said at these points to be of theological concern.

Certainly one of the sources of penetrating and most helpful insight in matters of this kind is the large place which is held by missions in the public life of these churches; not only by an awareness of the missionary imperative but also by missionary organizations and professional personnel. Such persons are proportionately more numerous, and find more of a hearing, than in the "mainstream" denominations. It is natural that persons with this kind of insight and commitment should learn to see the shortcomings of colonialism, cultural paternalism, racism, and nationalism in a way not everyone can. It is even possible for missionaries working in places such as Latin America to recognize that the only hope for these societies will be in some kind of "revolution" or some kind of change in economic structures. Thus the missionary experience and perspective break through the limits and the prejudices of the home churches in a redemptive way; it is no surprise that it is the missionary agencies which have been at the forefront of evangelical unity and social concern in the last decade.

There is a *growing theological perspective on the meaning of suffering.* To speak specifically of the peace churches, it is a most significant fact that the initial insight which led the first of them, the Swiss Brethren in 1525, to their rejection of killing and war was not a particular interpretation of a particular biblical text, but rather a profound understanding of what it means to share in the sufferings of Christ. Even before the first baptism and before it had become clear what shape the young Brethren movement was to take, Conrad Grebel wrote in 1524,

> . . . the Gospel and its adherents are not to be protected by the sword, nor are they thus to protect themselves. . . . True Christian believers are sheep among wolves, sheep for the slaughter; they must be baptized in anguish and afflic-

tion, tribulation, persecution, suffering, and death; they must be tried with fire, and must reach the fatherland of eternal rest, not by killing them bodily, but by mortifying their spiritual enemies. Neither do they use worldly sword nor war, since all killing has ceased with them; unless of course, we are still on the level of the Old Testament. . . .

A Postscript added:

. . . if thou must suffer for it, know well that it cannot be otherwise. Christ must suffer still more in His members. But He will strengthen them and keep them steadfast to the end. May God give grace to thee and us.[5]

We see here no naive prooftexting and no search for moral purity. This small circle of Zurich believers had seen what Jesus had meant when He spoke in the same terms of His cross and that of His disciples.

It is therefore a ground of hope, and a promise that we might be able to move beyond the fruitless exchange of proof texts and the unshaken commitment of each party to his hermeneutic assumptions, when we find this understanding of the suffering of the church once again clearly coming to the surface in evangelical mission thinking.

The last major paper at the Congress on the Church's World Wide Mission had to do with the situation of the church in a hostile world. The speaker was a man responsible for missionary work in the Congo.

When Christ called His disciples to Him, He "bade them come and die." He called them to lives of self-repudiation, self-denial. He called them to bear the cross and follow Him. This meant resisting "the crushing power of earthly lordships." This meant servanthood, bearing the yoke, and "learning obedience" by suffering (Matthew 11:29; Hebrews 5:8). "Only in the conflict of Christian labor is soul satisfaction found and only in hardship and sacrifice is the message of the Gospel made meaningful to a world suffering because of sin" (Kerr). Apostolic service in the New Testament involved "suffering in passion for the perfection of the Church and the accomplishment of its mission."

Some of the most profound passages in the New Testament are taken with this intimate association between conflict and mission, suffering and mission (e.g., Col. 1:24; 2:1). Apparently it is impossible to be spiritually fruitful without embracing this truth. This means that the hostility of the world is but the necessary context in which these spiritual principles can be implemented, to the glory of God and the blessing of mankind. "You cannot separate the mission and the passion in a universal Christianity. There is no world crown without the Cross. The Church that missions really dies with Christ, and its missionaries but show forth His death" (Forsyth).[6]

The same sentiments are expressed by Norman Grubb, the spiritual mentor of the Worldwide Evangelization Crusade, in an article which I must retranslate out of the Spanish since I have not seen it in the original English. Interpreting the meaning of missionary martyrdom in the Congo, he writes in an article entitled "It Is an Honor to Die for Christ":

All is joy. The cross is His glory. Our crosses, when the privilege of carrying them is given to us, are our glory through His glory. The culmination of love is to lay down our lives. He is love; and we in him are love. . . .
Why did I recount all of this [a story of martyrdom in the Congo]? It is the law of the harvest. Jesus said it centuries

ago. The grain of wheat must die. This is the means God uses. God in Christ likewise followed this path, and we are saved thereby. Will not the servant follow the path which the Master opened? This is love raised to the highest degree. For many it will mean the sacrifice of years of their life. For some few, the final abandonment. Martyrdom is implicit when we accept the honor of the calling of God.

We have now become accustomed in such a way to ease that when some of our co-laborers pay the total price we are dismayed. Let us gird up our loins and accept the fact that in the future the missionary calling will signify not safety but danger. It will take for granted not the superiority of white men, but service rendered with humility. But the harvest is sure. That we know.[7]

IV

Finally, I want to address the diversity and unity in institutional evangelicalism, which, as was briefly indicated earlier, has been handled in the distinction between essentials in which one must be in full agreement and nonessentials in which variety is permissible or even desirable. This distinction has been a major assumption in American fundamentalism and evangelicalism. If we may try to describe somewhat more precisely this attitude to the problem of diversity, its logic is made up of at least five elements.

1. It is possible to make clear distinction in kind between items of faith which are essential and those which are not. In making this assumption, fundamentalism, although perhaps the first movement to take its name from a particular choice of "fundamentals," was proceeding in a way which had been attempted before. Already Augustine had promulgated the vision of "agreement in essentials, diversity in non-essentials, and love in

all things." Roman Catholicism, Erasmian humanism, and theological liberalism as well have used such formulae.

2. It is clearly assumed that essential doctrinal agreement is the same thing as spiritual unity; on the other hand, a lack of essential agreement means there should be no sustained relationship between Christian groups. Nonessentials are defined precisely by the fact that when one differs at those points they do not stand in the way of spiritual unity.

3. The essentials are doctrinal matters; one does not find in this category issues of church order (which Roman Catholicism would find essential, or for which Anabaptists were persecuted) or of ethics (which might be essential to certain humanistic traditions).

4. Because the issue of war and the Christian attitude toward it is not an essential, Mennonites are welcome in the institutional cooperative agencies of American evangelicalism.

5. Because variety in nonessentials is a good thing, Mennonites should not make an issue of their attitude at this point, when gathered with other evangelicals for activities which express their essential unity. Because nonessentials do not prevent unity they need not be debated.

This distinction is held to be self-evident; that is both its strength and its weakness. Its self-evidence is its strength. In every kind of Christian group some such distinction is used, both to justify efforts at unity when it is felt that there is essential agreement, and to explain division when the disagreement is considered essential.

Any linguistic usage which is thus usually accepted must have something to it. I do not mean to deny the functional utility of such a distinction when in a given context it can be used responsibly. Yet the weakness of such a self-evident proposition is that if it *never* needs to be examined or challenged, and if it can with equal facility be used to defend almost any theological position, then it must be a distinction on the verbal rather than on the substantial level. One must then question whether it really provides as much guidance as is initially assumed; whether it perhaps remains convincing only so far as it is taken for granted. Especially does it seem challengeable when its implication for Mennonites attending evangelical meetings is that they should "go easy" on issues which seem to them to be of deep spiritual importance, at the same time that their collaboration is solicited for kinds of cooperation which, since they are in the minority, they have little capacity to help determine.

I propose therefore to argue, respectfully but with some vigor, that this self-evident distinction between the essential and the nonessential, for all the immediate promise it gives of helping us solve problems, is actually deceptive and theologically questionable.

All the major issues on which, since the Middle Ages, Christians have divided, for the sake of which some were ready to persecute and others to be persecuted, were questions not of doctrine but of church order or ethics. This was markedly the case for Mennonite forebears, the Anabaptists of the sixteenth century. All parties agreed that these Anabaptists were in full agreement with Luther and Zwingli on all of the matters which were considered *doctrinally* essential (the authority of the Bible, the sacrifical work of Christ, justification by faith . . .); and yet it was issues of church order (relationship of church and state), of sacramental practice (whether to baptize infants), and of ethics (the use of the sword and the oath), for the sake of which it was determined by the authoritative interpreters of Protestantism, especially Zwingli, Luther, and Calvin, and by the authoritative creedal documents of Protestantism, that Anabaptists were to be persecuted to the death. Certainly there is something historically questionable about an analysis which would have the Reformers calling on the Christian rulers to put people to death for issues which are not essential. In spite of the verbal distinction, the leaders of state church Protestantism must actually have believed that the maintenance of a state church and of infant baptism were sufficiently *essential* that it was worth killing dissenters to maintain them.

I question the distinction on the grounds of Christian statesmanship and brotherly relations. Matthew 18, one of the fundamental descriptions of the process of fraternal relations within the church, instructs us to begin the process of conversation in which Christ's presence is promised, around offense and not around agreement. The Anabaptists, and the other free churches in their train, including British Puritanism, and the American Restoration Movement, made much of a "theology of disputation," according to which it is through the free interchange of ideas within the brotherhood on points of major difference that truth can be made known more clearly.

In the New Testament story itself, the attitude of the Apostle Paul toward "Judaizers" was not one of readiness to let unity be defined by agreement and disunity by essential disagreement. He believed that the Judaizers were very deeply wrong, to the extent that he could say that they were preaching another gospel, or that they

were denying implicitly the work of Christ. Yet he did
not simply cut off relations with them; he made debate
with them a matter of major concern in the churches for
which he was responsible. He went the second mile to
maintain fellowship with the church at Jerusalem, which
he would not have had to do, thus assuming a kind of
continuing unity with those with whom he was not in
agreement about an essential item.

Certainly it is true that for a certain kind of collaboration in concrete activity, there must be sufficient
agreement to permit that collaboration to be clear and
honest. What is "essential" in this pragmatic sense is defined only practically; to do a job together you must be
desirous of doing the same job. But there is according to
the New Testament also a clear responsibility for the
brother with whom one disagrees, including the brother
with whom one disagrees essentially, which is just as
binding as the obligation to collaborate in common
projects, if not more so. The biblical interpretation of difference is not that it is tolerable when nonessential and
intolerable when essential. It is rather that the more important the difference is, the more binding is our obligation to work at it.

In all charity one must remark at this point that the
tendency of organized evangelical cooperation in recent
decades, to avoid debate at points of difference, in order
to collaborate in mutual respect in points of agreement,
is but another shading of the kind of "inclusivism" of
which the larger ecumenical movement is so often ac-
cused. It is the World Council of Churches (not to as
great an extent the National Council in the USA) which
provides formally structured ways of carrying on debate
about issues where varying groups differ widely. The

World Council puts differences on the agenda; the NAE avoids discussing them in order to discuss only common emphases.

I challenge on New Testament grounds the idea that doctrine is more essential than church order or ethics. Jesus' own words, "Why call ye me Lord, Lord?" have in the past history of evangelicalism rightly been clearly understood as relativizing creedal orthodoxy, when looked at for its own sake. This is not to say that doctrine is unimportant or a matter of indifference; but evangelicalism until this century has always argued that correct teaching is not a source of real security for the church or the individual believer. Since in the latter part of the last century evangelicalism and creedal orthodoxy made common cause against the rising threat of modernism, evangelical thinkers are less critical at this point, and it would seem less biblical, than they used to be. But unfortunately, by thus joining in an alliance against modernism, evangelicalism and creedalism have also joined in a not fully conscious alliance against the Anabaptist and the Holiness traditions. It therefore needs to continue to be argued that "doing the things that I say" is according to Jesus, part of the criterion of faithfulness, and that creedal correctness can be a cover for apostasy.

With regard to our present problem, this is demonstrated by the way in which evangelicalism has taken over almost unconsciously and quite uncritically the entire body of thought represented by the traditional doctrine of the just war. Not only those theological conservatives who would be happy to say that they lean upon the Westminster Confession or the Heidelberg Catechism, but also most of those who depreciate the value of formal creeds, would still structure their thought around the problem of war according to the logic of the just war theory. And yet this is a theory from the age of Constantine, when the church and the world were identical, when the most important Christian in the nation was the prince, when the gospel demand and promise of conversion and the formation of visible groups of believers were not part of the picture at all.

The very capacity of evangelicalism thus to incorporate unconsciously a major part of the ethical thought of medieval apostasy is a sign of what happens when ethics is declared to be outside the realm of *essential* theological concern. Modern evangelicals are, therefore, at this point according to the inner structure of their thought and its sociological presuppositions, not really evangelicals, committed to all the implications of individual faith and the voluntary church, but rather theocrats, concerned for the maintenance of a Protestant Christendom in which the throne and the pulpit are allied. This realm of ethical thought has not been changed (as it logically should have been) by consideration of the character of the new nature imparted to the believer by regeneration, nor have any of the implications of the fact that the free church is a missionary minority in the hostile world been drawn out. This alliance is well demonstrated by the fact that *Christianity Today* can cite the Westminister Confession (which specifically rejects the Anabaptists' concern for the believers' church) as a document on contemporary social ethics, by which to evaluate whether statements of ecumenical study groups on social concerns are theologically acceptable.

Another point at which this criticism of the non-essentiality of ethics needs to be focused is the special teaching of Jesus about the place of the cross of the Christian. Jesus does not say about his celibacy or His way of dressing or His itineration that every disciple must imitate Him. He does however say that whoever would be His disciple must bear a cross. This means, to foreshorten the argument, that what Jesus does about human conflict, human community, and social power is normative for His disciple in a way that other aspects of His example and His teaching are not. Even if it could be argued that some elements of ethical concern are not essential (such as celibacy or whether to own property), it would still have to be said on New Testament grounds that the matter of violence and enmity in social relations is a special case.

Whether then we look at the logic of the peace church position, as based on the full meaning of the work of Christ for Christian discipleship, or at the present conversational situation in the conservative-evangelical world, or at the validity of the kinds of reasoning whereby more serious dealing with this issue has been detoured hitherto, the conclusion is the same: it is the peace churches' duty, not as a dead heritage but as a gospel message, to communicate more insistently and more convincingly with regard to the Christian attitude to war. How can this most fittingly be done?

6

CHURCH GROWTH PRINCIPLES AND CHRISTIAN DISCIPLESHIP

Richard Showalter

An interest in numerical church growth and a commitment to costly discipleship are not contradictory. Quality and quantity go together in God's intention for evangelism. The Great Commission of Matthew 28 clearly says, "Make disciples of *all* nations," and "Teach them to observe *all* things." "All nations" indicates God's concern for quantity; "all things" attests His concern for quality.

Jesus consistently cared about both. The very word "discipleship" comes to us from His patient commitment to a small group of men and women who carried on His mission after Pentecost. Yet His commitment to the multitudes, His compassion for the crowds, never wavered. He never moved into a corner to create an island of purity in isolation from the world. He came *to the world* (John 3:16).

The Acts of the Apostles contains many references to church growth.[1] We may without apology cite Acts as a manual of case studies in early church growth. In contrast, the Epistles are "follow-up letters." Their focus is nurture for discipleship, addressed specifically to young Christians in young churches.

Thus we discover in the Great Commission, in the ministry of Jesus, and in the remainder of the New Testament a balanced concern for numerical church growth and for discipleship; an explicit assumption that winning the unbeliever and discipling the believer are equally expressions of God's will for the church. The gospel is good news for believer and unbeliever alike. Any other gospel is not the "gospel of God" (Romans 1:1).

Consequently we may expect the norms of Christian discipleship to serve as checks on our understanding of church growth and the norms of church growth to check our understanding of discipleship. A non-evangelistic discipleship is not New Testament discipleship. A church growth that is not serious about discipleship is not New Testament church growth.

I

What is "church growth"? A wave of interest in principes of church growth has engulfed evangelical churches and missionary agencies in North America in recent years. Much of the language and theory of church growth in a semi-technical sense has originated with the teaching and writing of Donald McGavran of the School of World Mission at Fuller Theological Seminary and has been developed in a variety of ways by his colleagues there. In this paper we will take a major church growth principle, the homogeneous unit principle, as it has been set forth by these church growth teachers and ask how it is checked by a concern for true discipleship.

The spirit of Anabaptism was missionary. In the twentieth century we have lifted up many different characteristics of the Anabaptist movement—discipleship, peace, and the nature of the church. Although these have often held center stage, the missionary character of Anabaptism is inescapable. The early Anabaptists never thought of themselves as an isolated minority, witnessing in the backwaters of Christendom, but rather as the true church, responsible for carrying the apostolic gospel into all the world. As Menno Simons himself wrote, "He sent out His messengers preaching this peace, His apostles who spread this grace abroad through the whole world, who shone as bright, burning torches before all men, so that they might lead me and all erring sinners into the right way. ... Their words I love, their practices I follow."[2]

Historically then the understanding of discipleship was formed in a missionary matrix. Whenever it is separated from that matrix, from an evangelistic "church growth" motivation, it is likely to be misunderstood. Conversely, it is also true that the strong Anabaptist orientation to the believers' church and to suffering love gave a particular shape to the way in which they evangelized. Thus in the Anabaptist movement we see an integrated expression of church growth and discipleship which is very similar to that which we observed in the New Testament.

Are present-day Mennonites true brothers and sisters of their Anabaptist ancestors? Do they express and experience the same balanced commitment to evangelistic discipleship that we see in the pages of the New

Testament? These questions have been asked and answered in many different ways. Here I would like to make only two observations.

(1) The Anabaptist movement was more like "home missions" than like "foreign missions." The Anabaptists witnessed primarily to their cultural and geographic neighbors.

(2) Although the Mennonite Church has had some organizations for mission, we have not been part of such a hometown evangelistic movement since the sixteenth century. The Mennonite Church as we know it has not been part of movements like the Anabaptist, the Wesleyan, or those reported in the Acts of the Apostles. Many explanations could be given for this—spiritual, sociological, political, or psychological explanations. Whatever the explanation, it is clear that the part of Mennonite theology which seems to us most "Anabaptist" (discipleship, peace, the nature of the church) comes to us from a missionary context which is quite distinct from the context in which we find ourselves today. This fact gives special importance to contemporary discussions of both evangelism and discipleship, reminding us that our perspectives are likely to need constant adjustment in both of these areas.

II

With this background, I want to present several basic assumptions relating to church growth. *Current evangelical church growth theory is practical, not speculative.* Missionaries, pastors, and mission board secretaries get excited (or turned off) by it. It is an attempt to describe systematically why some churches grow and others do not. If a church is growing and someone observes, "That church is growing in defiance of the principles of church growth," the church growth researcher simply says, "There are reasons for its growth. When I understand them they will become part of church growth theory."

Church growth theology is the theology of the person who is studying church growth. If the researcher is theologically trained, he may carefully attach his church growth theory to a particular theological system. If not, he may assume the validity of his own theology and depreciate theology in general. Developing church growth theory only demands that a person care enough about helping churches to grow that he is willing to examine why churches grow. The most important link between church growth theory and a theology will lie in the motivations and reasons which that theology provides for church growth and the responsibility which that theology lays on Christians to help God grow churches. If a theology does not encourage church growth, or if it assumes that human beings have nothing to do with working at church growth, such a theology will obviously undercut interest in church growth. On questions such as these, church growth theorists always become "theological."

Church growth theory is at home in a cultural setting which is "scientific" and "descriptive." In North America everything is described sociologically, anthropologically, or psychologically. In evangelism we follow suit by providing "scientific descriptions" of why churches grow. Scientific description is not in itself bad, but it does not tell us whether any particular church growth is "good growth." Church growth principles as formulated by Donald McGavran and others assume a broad evangelical consensus on the fact that God wills church growth and that it is possible for us all to recognize "good growth" without much debate.

Intrinsically, none of this either threatens or encourages a strong peace witness.

III

"Birds of a feather flock together ..." is common folk knowledge. "Men like to become Christians without crossing racial, linguistic, or class barriers."[3] This statement by McGavran implies the most controversial principle of church growth theory. One can then go on to say, "Let them do it. Present the gospel within their cultural system so that they do not need to cross any such barriers. They will become Christians more readily." This is sometimes called the "homogeneous unit principle." "The homogeneous unit is simply a section of society in which all the members have some characteristic in common."[4] Since "birds of a feather flock together," and since communication is easier and more accurate within such homogeneous units, churches planted within a homogeneous unit will appeal more readily to unbelievers within that unit than will churches within a different social or cultural context.

For the missionary this means two things: (1) launching new fellowships will be easier if these fellowships appeal culturally and socially to a particular group of people or section of society, and (2) the more the evangelist is able to identify with those to whom he is ministering, the easier will be the launching of new fellowships.

It would be difficult to reject these statements as a sociological insight. They are descriptively valid. They constantly influence local churches in their operation and membership. On the most fundamental level, they mean that an English-speaking Christian will fellowship most readily with other English-speaking Christians if they are available rather than choosing those who speak only Swahili. In Ohio it means that people who come from southern Appalachia are attracted to churches with patterns of worship and communication which are like those "back home." Sociologically this is the "way things are." Church growth theory which stresses the homogeneous unit principle as a principle to be applied to promote growth is taking us one step further. Church growth theory says, in effect, "Since we all act in this way, let us use our knowledge of that fact to create clear communication of the gospel, to provide settings in which people can really, truly 'hear' the gospel, hear it in their own language, thought patterns, and social context." As a principle to be applied, this is simply a matter of elementary (but important) communications theory. Effective communicators, whether Christian missionaries or not, try to share their message intelligibly and clearly with every public or private audience they have. In order to communicate they must "speak their language."

What has this to do with discipleship? A lot! Two distinct applications emerge immediately. First, the homogeneous unit principle seems logical and scriptural. The more clearly we communicate the gospel, the more readily the issues of discipleship will be grasped by new Christians. Outside my social and cultural context, my "truth" may become someone else's untruth, simply because what I *meant* is not what was *heard*. (This can, of course, happen even within my own family, but it is not as likely because the cultural distance is less.) We illustrate the problem when we say, "You have to take a

Dutchman by what he means, not by what he says."

In this way, by encouraging church growth within specific homogeneous units, we make faithful discipleship more likely to occur. We increase the likelihood that more and more people within that world (homogeneous unit) will truly understand the gospel. Conversely, if a person meets Christ primarily outside his own "world" in someone else's cultural setting, Christ and His way of peace are more likely to seem foreign and unattractive. When the way of peace is presented and actually lived by one's neighbors at home it is not as easy to shake off and dismiss. The history of the peace churches since the Reformation testifies eloquently to this principle.

Second, however, *we must not take a principle of communication and make it an ecclesiological norm.* If we should do so, we would become guilty of sin against the unity of the body of Christ and we would substitute human community for divine community. All of our discipling would then be compromised. To make this principle an ecclesiological norm would be to reason as follows:

1. Homogeneous churches grow more rapidly.
2. All churches should grow more rapidly.
3. Therefore all churches should be culturally and socially homogeneous.

This logic might make sense if we were thinking only of numerical growth, although even then there might be problems. However, although numerical growth is one worthy goal, it is combined in the New Testament with "teaching them all things." To use an extreme example we do not really believe that Buddhist churches should grow more rapidly. Nor do we really believe that *all* Christian churches should grow faster all of the time. If rapid church growth is actually the rapid growth of heresy (e.g., racism, syncretism) then the concern for maturity in Christ takes precedence. If rapid growth is merely producing more babies who are not being fed and therefore must die in infancy, then it is not good growth.

The crucial distinction is this: a homogeneous unit church which has been planted by design by Christian apostles or evangelists as a missionary community will be a natural setting in which true discipleship can be fostered. This is genuine, biblical church growth. The principle of homogeneity can and should be applied as a norm for communication both at home and abroad. It contributes both to numerical church growth and to growth in discipleship, including the peace witness. But, if "birds of a feather flock together" becomes a norm of ecclesiology, if *inside* a local church fellowship we use homogeneity as a principle of exclusion rather than as a principle of communication, we pave the way for all kinds of aberrations in discipleship—nationalism, racism, and various forms of party spirit.

IV

In summary, the following are presented:

(1) Interest in numerical church growth and commitment to costly discipleship are not mutually exclusive.

(2) Promoting numerical growth within homogeneous units, producing "homogeneous unit churches," is good mission strategy provided young Christians are not taught that the church *should* be homogeneous, taught that other Christians who are in some way not like us should not be welcomed as part of us.

(3) An insight which describes the way things are (such as "birds of a feather flock together") can be utilized as good mission strategy for the promotion of church growth, for facilitating the communication of the gospel *into* a new situation; but can be bad if it is used as a statement of the way things ought to be, from the inside looking out.

(4) Two rules for the evangelist-missionary: (a) Reject the comfort of homogeneity for self; be ready to identify with all kinds of people for the sake of Christ. (b) Accept others as our Lord receives them, without demanding any cultural dislocation on their part; some day they will have the same privilege.

7

MENNONITE MISSIONS AND THE CHRISTIAN PEACE WITNESS

Robert L. Ramseyer

> The regenerate, therefore lead a penitent and new life, for they are renewed in Christ and have received a new heart and spirit. ... They are the children of peace who have beaten their swords into plowshares and their spears into pruning hooks, and know war no more.—Menno Simons, *The New Birth*.

The Mennonite tradition, springing as it does from the pacifist segment of the radical Reformation, has always taught that Christians must not take part in war and the killing of human beings. For this reason, Mennonites have frequently come into conflict with national governments and have migrated from country to country seeking places where they may be permitted to practice their faith in peace. Mennonites have also been active in the modern missionary movement, particularly in the twentieth century, and their missionaries have founded Mennonite churches in Africa, Asia, and Latin America. However, in most cases, these more recently founded Mennonite churches have not been "peace churches" in the way in which the older churches from which missionaries were sent had been. In this chapter we will seek to:

(1) Examine the Mennonite missionary record on the peace witness very briefly.

(2) Examine the reasons for the separation of salvation and the peace witness in Mennonite missions.

(3) Show that salvation in Jesus Christ and the way of peace are inseparable.

(4) Make some suggestions as to what this may mean for the Mennonite missionary today.

I

With few exceptions, Mennonite churches founded by Mennonite missionaries as part of the modern missionary movement lack a distinctive peace witness. They are in almost all essentials like churches founded by evangelical Protestant missionaries from Europe and North America. In their own self-understanding missionary-founded Mennonite churches are evangelical Protestant, bearing the name Mennonite only as a kind of historical link to the churches from which the missionaries came. These churches are so standardly Protestant in character that in some parts of the world Mennonite missionaries have taken over already existing churches founded by Baptist or other missions without feeling any need for making significant changes in the understanding which these churches had as to what it means to be a follower of Jesus Christ in this world. In some countries, Mennonite

missionaries have hired pastors from other churches and
traditions to pastor Mennonite churches, again apparently without requiring radical change in the understanding which the pastors have of what it means to be a
Christian. In each case a change of name to "Mennonite" has been sufficient.

It is true that in some Mennonite churches founded by
missionaries, leaders do understand that the churches
which sent the missionaries teach peace and counsel their
own church members to reject participation in their
country's military activities. However both the
missionary-founded churches and the missionaries seem
to feel that the peace teaching and the rejection of the
military way are ethical decisions which are not part of
the gospel message. They may be a higher and more
perfect way of following Jesus, but they are not a basic
and essential element in the way of Christ. Thus in
Brazil, the head of the Mennonite conference can be a
career military officer; in Taiwan Mennonite seminary
students serve their terms in the armed forces; in India
the military may be perceived as a legitimate way for a
poor Christian to earn a better wage; and in Indonesia
and Zaire Mennonites may see no contradiction between
their Christian faith and the military defense of their new
nations. Even in Japan where the Mennonite Church
does take the biblical peace position, this stand is
probably due more to the general cultural receptivity to
peace and to the Japanese church leaders having been
students of the Anabaptist heritage, than to any new
understanding of the relationship between the peace witness and the task of Mennonite missionaries.

In summary, most Mennonite churches founded by
missionaries have had little or no peace witness because,

correctly or incorrectly, most Mennonite missionaries apparently did not include the peace witness as an important part of their presentation of the gospel.

II

A gospel without a peace witness is not a new phenomenon in church history. The roots of this Mennonite missionary problem go back at least to the early centuries of the Christian church. Early in the life of the church creeds were written which began to make statements about the nature of Jesus. Threatened by heresies which would have reduced Jesus to an exceptional human being, the church needed to define His nature more precisely. However, over the centuries the definitions of His nature, "the only begotten Son of God, begotten of His Father before all worlds, God of God, Light of Light, Very God of Very God, begotten, not made, being of one substance with the Father, by whom all things were made," came to be more important than who Jesus is as a living Person. In venerating Jesus as the Son of God, Christians tended to lose sight of the fact that He is the living active Son of God whose worship must include following Him in the way that they live. In worship Christians tended to follow the example of Peter on the Mount of Transfiguration and forgot that Jesus took His disciples down off the mountain and that worship includes both separated times of adoration and living under Jesus' leadership in ordinary life as well. It became easy to think of Jesus primarily as a sort of religious object to be manipulated for salvation rather than as a living Person to be followed in a Lord-disciple relationship. However, the self-revelation of God in the Bible is that He is never an object, He is I AM, eternally the Actor, the subject. This is the significant difference between what He asks of His followers and what goes on in most religious traditions. It was the genius of some of the early Anabaptists that they were able to see that the Christ of the creeds is the Lord to be followed in all of life. This emphasis on *living* the Christian life, with all of the dangers of moralism and self-righteousness which it contains, became the Mennonite understanding of what it means to be a Christian.

Nevertheless, the evidence is clear that Mennonite missions did not begin primarily from this understanding of the gospel. Rather the missionary impetus came from the impact of the evangelical revival on Mennonite churches. Moved by revival, many acculturating Mennonites became convinced that the traditional Mennonite emphasis had become a dead moralistic legalism without an inner experience with Jesus Christ. Reacting against this background, many came then to emphasize the spiritual regeneration which they felt had been lacking in their own heritage and relegated to a secondary position an emphasis on following Jesus in every aspect of daily life. Obviously these categories are not mutually exclusive, and evangelical Protestants and Mennonites have always included both in their understanding of the faith. However, for Mennonites in missions there had come a definite shift in emphasis.

> No longer was the very content of salvation to be found in yieldedness, obedience and discipleship, living separated as God's people, living by the love ethic, and depending humbly on Christ (however much the fathers had distorted these).[1]

This shift does not mean that Mennonite missionaries

and those who sent and supported them had given up the peace witness. It does mean that they had come to see the gospel as a body of beliefs to be accepted in order to achieve a spiritual salvation, a salvation which could be followed, as new Christians grew in spiritual maturity, with a variety of ethical teachings about the committed Christian life, including the Mennonite teaching on peace and nonresistance.

> For Mennonites salvation and release from human sin were no longer to come by the very living of the new life to which God had called, and to which Jesus by his self-sacrifice had shown the way.[2]

The New Testament call to "believe in the Lord Jesus and you will be saved" came to be understood as synonymous with "believe that Jesus died for you and that His blood washes away your sins; accept Him as your Savior and you will be saved." Mennonites in mission understood themselves as being evangelical Protestants with some unique additions, including the peace witness.

Most Christians concerned about the basic missionary task would probably agree that evangelism and church planting have higher priority for the foreign missionary than do the long-term pastoring and teaching of people who are already Christians. The place of the peace witness in missions then depends on how we understand salvation and becoming a Christian. If our image of conversion is limited to the spiritual act of opening the doors of our hearts and saying, "Come in, Lord Jesus," then the peace witness will logically be the work of pastors and teachers who follow the missionary. If however we understand salvation and becoming a Christian as a turning around in all of life, if we understand the presence of Jesus in the heart as an empowering for change from not following Jesus in the way we live to following Him, then obviously the way of peace will be part of that initial evangelistic witness since who Jesus is and the road that He leads us on are inextricably bound up with the way of peace.

Sometimes Mennonites have seen the peace witness as a Mennonite distinctive which they are not sure should be required of Christians in other countries at all. They see it as a unique vocation for one peculiar strand of Christian people, not a characteristic of all Christians. Certainly many good non-Mennonite missionaries see their peace church colleagues in this way. I well remember the incredulity of one missionary after I had read a paper at a study conference in Japan when it suddenly dawned on him that "he really believes that this is for *all* Christians!"

Mennonite missionary writings show plainly that most missionaries felt that first people must experience Christ in their hearts. After they have personally experienced Him, then they can be taught and will understand the biblical teaching on peace. Somehow it was thought to be possible to experience Jesus Christ in one's heart without knowing at all what this means for the most basic human relationships. Missionaries had retained an orthodox creedal understanding of Jesus as the Son of God, but somehow had separated the experience of regeneration in Christ from the purpose of regeneration—power to live as His disciple in all of life.

Given this understanding of the relationship between the gospel of salvation and the peace witness, a number of reasons can be listed for the almost total neglect of the peace teaching on some mission fields.

(1) In some areas missionaries were so continually confronted by the presence of multitudes of unsaved people that they never felt able to leave the preaching of salvation to take up many of the other things which were seen as the possible fruit of salvation. "The missionary found so many elementary things that needed to be taught to the young Christians as a minimum doctrine for salvation and for mere survival in their Christian life that the tenet of non-resistance as we think of it in the homeland could hardly receive special attention. The average 'heathen Christian' has only a very faint or no understanding of its full scope."[3]

(2) Many missionaries worked in colonial lands among native people who were not eligible for military service. Therefore they saw no immediate necessity of teaching this particular derivative implication of the Christian life.

(3) Many missionaries felt that such "ethical details" should be left to the newly emerging churches to define in their own cultural context as they became more mature.

(4) The peace witness is the one aspect of the Christian life in which otherwise law-abiding Christians are likely to confront their societies and their governments. Teaching this position may make the Christian faith unpopular and the gathering of converts more difficult. Moreover in some situations faithful adherence may mean imprisonment or death for the Christian. Out of genuine love and concern, missionaries from abroad hesitate to ask new converts to take this kind of risk. Secondarily, missionaries realize that teaching this position may mean their own expulsion from the country, ending missionary activity.

(5) Today most missionaries have gone from the imperialistic nations of the West to the newly emerging nations of the so-called Third World. Because they are perceived as agents of their own societies, an antimilitary posture in the mission field may be perceived as an attempt by the imperialists to keep the new nations weak and open to exploitation. They may also be seen as agents trying to weaken the new national identity by forcing Christians to have divided loyalties.

Many other reasons could be listed. Papers by Graber, Pannabecker, and Janzen on "Nonresistance and Missions" presented to the Mennonite Central Committee Peace Section Study Conference in November 1950 list a wide variety. The important point here is that these are reasonable only if one begins with an understanding that makes the way of peace a fruit, perhaps an important fruit, of the gospel, but not an essential part of the gospel itself. But this understanding of salvation deserves greater study as I propose to do in the next section.

III

What is our missionary task? Most Christians have probably understood our missionary task as a fulfillment of the Great Commission, "Go, then, to all peoples everywhere and make them my disciples: baptize them in the name of the Father, the Son, and the Holy Spirit, and teach them to obey everything I have commanded" (Matthew 28:19, 20, TEV). This leads to a second question.

What is a disciple of Jesus Christ and how does a person become one? What does it mean to be a Christian? Are salvation and living as a disciple of Jesus Christ one thing or two separate things? Many of us today find it difficult to accept what the New Testament actually says about salvation because we are afraid that we might fall into the trap of preaching a message of salvation on the basis of works instead of salvation by the grace of God alone.

It is unfortunate that our thinking about what it means to be a disciple of Jesus Christ has become confused with disputations about faith and works. In trying to understand what Paul means when he says, "For it is by God's grace that you have been saved through faith. It is not the result of your own effort, but God's gift" (Ephesians 2:8, TEV), we need to remember for whom he was writing. Paul's letters were sent to people who were familiar with the Old Testament and what it meant to be saved in the world of the Old Testament. In this world salvation was a way of life, in which being saved was closely related to how one lived here and now. But these people also lived in a world in which the Old Testament way of the covenant people had been perverted into a rigid legalism. People thought that they could, by zealously observing a set of rules, maneuver God into blessing them. In this situation Paul says, "Wait. You don't maneuver God into doing anything. God is the Lord. If God accepts you, it is only by His gracious will, not because of anything you have done to impress Him with your goodness."

Salvation by faith alone in the Pauline sense has nothing to do with a separation of salvation from a way of life with Jesus Christ. It is certainly not meant to make salvation a spiritual experience independent of the way in which we live. James is making precisely this point when he declares that there is no such thing as faith divorced from works. Faith without the Christian life cannot in fact exist. The fact that he felt compelled to make the point would seem to indicate that this misunderstanding of salvation goes back to the very first century of the church.

The Christian life is a loving response to a loving God, a way of life made possible by the power of His Spirit at work within the Christian disciple, but it is not only to please God that we try to live in this way. If that were all that discipleship were, then it might indeed be only a fruit of salvation. Rather, the Christian life is itself the life of salvation; it is being saved. In many discussions of evangelism and mission, salvation has been twisted until it refers almost entirely to what happens after physical death, and the fact that Christian discipleship is itself the state of being saved while we are here in this world has often been forgotten. When this happens, discipleship becomes a difficult task, an ethical duty designed to please or impress God, instead of the joyful salvation for which we have been created, for which His Spirit gives power, and for which the entire world yearns. Living as a disciple of Jesus Christ is living in this world in the way in which we were created to live. Being a disciple of Jesus Christ means living in the peace of God. It is salvation itself.

This vision of the New Testament mission was what the Anabaptists recovered and most Mennonites lost again. It is a vision of what it means to be a Christian which is very different from that which was held by the Reformers and their spiritual descendants.

When Anabaptists went forth as missionaries, it was not primarily to spread a body of abstract belief, and certainly not to impose faith by political means and coercion. Rather they went forth with an invitation to a new kind of living in a new kind of group: as serious, suffering disciples in God's visible new community.[4]

What then about the people who claim faith in Jesus Christ but do go to war? Are they Christians? Are they disciples of Jesus Christ? Are they saved? Both the New Testament and its Anabaptist interpreters said clearly that salvation is very closely related to discipleship, to the way that one lives. "If you love me, you will obey my commandments" (John 14:15, TEV). "Not everyone who calls me 'Lord, Lord' will enter in the Kingdom of heaven, but only those who do what my Father in heaven wants them to do" (Matthew 7:21, TEV). "I warn you now as I have before: those who do these things will not possess the Kingdom of God" (Galatians 5:21, TEV). Hans Denck said, "Faith is the obedience to God,"[5] and "No one can know Christ unless he follow him in life."[6] Peter Rideman said, "There is therefore no need for many words, for it is clear that Christians can neither go to war nor practice vengeance. Whosoever doeth this hath forsaken and denied Christ and Christ's nature."[7]

No matter how uncomfortable and narrow this may make Christians feel in their relationships with evangelical friends, the meaning seems to be very plain. Obedience to Jesus Christ in our lives and salvation are very closely tied together. As Christ's followers we have been set free to obey Him, to follow in His way. It was surely no accident that the earliest followers of the Christian faith were not known as adherents of a new philosophy, but were known as followers of *The Way*. A disciple of Jesus Christ is one who follows in His way with His people.

Who is Jesus Christ? How do we understand Jesus Christ and our relationship to Him? Do we come to Him as person to thing, worshiper to sacred object, or do we come as person to Person, disciple to Lord? The tendency to depersonalize Jesus is seen most clearly when Jesus' death is interpreted exclusively in a transactional way— Jesus in His death paid a spiritual price which more than balanced human sin in God's record books through a spiritual transaction which took place far from the everyday world in which we live as human beings. When we lose sight of the fact that this transactional interpretation is only one of several biblical understandings of this action which Jesus took within human history, Jesus no longer stands as a Leader for us to follow, and the crucifixion no longer stands as a guide for us in determining how we are to live in this world.

In the Bible it is very clear that Jesus' death is very closely tied to who He was as a Person and how He lived as a Person. Jesus died on the cross because in His life He was perceived as a very distinct threat to powerful people and institutions in the society in which He lived. His way of life, the way of life which *is* salvation, was a way which was so threatening that it had to end on the cross. This is the Jesus who is our Lord. This is the Jesus whom we are called to follow as disciples. This is the Jesus who says that our mission is to make other disciples for Him. Being saved is being a disciple of Jesus Christ, and being a disciple of Jesus Christ is going the way that He went. How else can we interpret His words about taking up the cross and following Him? Or His words about only finding life when one has lost it?

In His sermon on the day of Pentecost, Peter is not talking about a depersonalized spiritual transaction.

"You killed him by letting sinful men nail him to the cross ... [but] God has made him Lord and Messiah." Stephen said, "You have betrayed and murdered him." Read Peter's message to Cornelius or look at the hymn in Paul's letter to the Philippians, chapter 2:6-11.

> He always had the nature of God,
> but he did not think that by force he
>   should try to become equal with God.
> Instead of this, of his own free will he gave up all
>   he had,
>   and took the nature of a servant.
> He became like man
>   and appeared in human likeness.
> He was humble and walked the path of
>   obedience all the way to death—
>   his death on the cross.
> For this reason God raised him to the
>   highest place above
> and gave him the name that is greater
>   than any other name.
> And so, in honor of the name of Jesus
>   all beings in heaven, on earth, and in the
>   world below
>   will fall on their knees,
> and all will openly proclaim that Jesus
>   Christ is the Lord,
> to the glory of God the Father.

Here the importance of who Jesus is as a Person is very clear. Because He became a human Servant, because He walked the path of salvation obediently all the way to the cross, because of who He is and what He did as a Person, God has made Him our Lord. Jesus is Someone to be committed to, Someone to follow. This leaves no possi-

bility of having faith in the Jesus Christ who is revealed
in the New Testament without being committed to walk-
ing where He walked in the way of peace, because the
Jesus Christ of the New Testament is a real Person who
lived and walked in the same world in which we have
been placed. " . . . Our life in this world is the same as
Christ's" (1 John 4:17, TEV). The depersonalized sa-
cralized Jesus Christ in whom one can believe and be
saved and only later, if at all, follow in life, is not the
same Jesus Christ at all.

This is our faith, and it is for this reason that the Council of Mission Board Secretaries (Mennonite and Brethren in Christ) meeting on September 30, 1959, could
adopt the following statement about the relationship of
the peace witness to our missionary task.

> We consider the message of peace a significant and inte-
> gral part of the evangelical faith. We share very deeply the
> conviction that our peace testimony must be clear in today's
> world, particularly in light of the threat of militarism and
> the surge of nationalism.
>
> A peace witness in a given country becomes the interest
> and concern of the Mennonite missions and churches in that
> country in order to effectively integrate the message of
> peace with the total message of the church and to assure this
> witness a solid evangelical foundation and expression. The
> establishment and operation of a peace witness therefore
> should primarily be the responsibility of the respective
> Mennonite mission boards and churches.

IV

The gospel has important implications for the nature
of the church of today. Because of almost 2,000 years of
church history and the nature of the world in which we

now live, the peace witness needs to receive far more emphasis in our missionary message than it would if we were beginning afresh in a world which had never heard of Christians. The message of peace is probably the aspect of the gospel which has been violated most frequently and most consistently by those who have called themselves Christians. As a result, in many parts of the world, in the minds of many people, the words "Christian" or "Jesus Christ" bring visions not of peace but of crusades, of the military might of the Western world, of the trampling boots of oppressing armies. In India, for example, people are well aware of the Christian soldiers from Britain and what they did to the Indian people. The walls of the Anglican cathedral in Calcutta are lined with plaques lauding the sacrifices of "Christian" British officers who gave their lives fighting the "heathen" people of India. Because of this heritage, the message of peace in the Christian gospel needs to be singled out for special attention merely in order to open the way for people to get back to who Christ really is and what He is really like, not the God of the Christian soldier, but the Prince of Peace. This same situation prevails almost anywhere in our world today. In a paper presented to the conjoint Council of Mission Board Secretaries/Mennonite Central Committee meeting on May 1, 1959, Melvin Gingerich said,

The realistic missionary must be aware of these misconceptions and must make his purposes and motivations crystal clear so that all will understand that he is not committed to the military program of the West, but is first, foremost, and always an ambassador of Christ. Needless to say this requires from us as Christ's representatives in the

Orient a very clear presentation of our peace conviction as part of our evangelistic message. To preach Christ is to invite the unconverted to come to him for salvation and to become his disciples. To extend the call to faith and discipleship to the unconverted demands that we explain what is involved in being a disciple. We cannot clarify discipleship without explaining what it means to take up the cross and follow Christ in all human relationships. This involves presenting him as the Prince of Peace when we call for faith in him.[8]

Even though it may make us seem narrow, unfriendly, and unecumenical, we need to come again to the spirit of those Anabaptists who said very clearly and boldly that regenerated people *do not* go to war, Christians *cannot* go to war. The Anabaptists were in a world very much like our own in which people who called themselves Christians rejected Christ's clear teaching on love and peace and associated a military posture with the Christian faith. The New Testament itself did not need to speak as boldly and as explicitly on the subject because in the world of the New Testament anyone who knew about Christ and Christians knew that they did not go to war, that peace and love were integral parts of the faith.

If we are faithful in this way we will need to face very squarely the fact that missionaries and local Christians may be very unpopular with the governments of the countries in which they live. In many parts of the world today the peace witness will be the key issue on which the basis of our ultimate loyalty will be tested. Do we give to the state the loyalty which it demands or do we give to God the loyalty which God demands? This is not a new situation. In the world of the New Testament the test of loyalty was over the deification of the emperor, but the issue of ultimate allegiance was the same and the testimony of the Christians was clear. Missionaries and local Christians were quite prepared to go underground rather than compromise. They did not reason that because faithfulness might mean the end of their public ministry they should compromise on this issue so as to be able to win more people for Christ. They were faithful, they went underground, people responded, and the church grew. Underground missions in which missionaries risk their lives are not much known today. Rather we talk of closed doors as if governmental disapproval automatically meant the end of missions. We might well look again and ask ourselves whether our only alternatives in some situations really are limited to unfaithfulness to the gospel of peace or the end of our mission witness.

If we are serious about the peace witness, then we will need to broaden our understanding of its implications far beyond the traditional area of direct participation in military activities. In our world today probably the area which most cries out for such attention is the economic realm and those institutional features of it which have been termed structural violence. Far too little has been done on this in Mennonite missionary circles. A notable exception is a paper presented by John Driver to the Mennonite Missionary Study Fellowship in 1975 entitled "The Anabaptist Vision and Social Justice."[9] A conference called by MCC Peace Section in 1950 expressed concern in this area.

> Parallel with this we must practice an increasingly sharper Christian control of our economic, social, and cultural practices among ourselves and toward others, to

make certain that love truly operates to work no ill to our neighbor, either short range or long range. Knowing how much the selfishness, pride, and greed of individuals, groups, and nations, which economic systems often encourage, help to cause strife and warfare, we must see to it that we do not contribute thereto, whether for the goals of direct military operations or to anything which destroys property or causes hurt or loss of human life.[10]

In our missionary message what do we say about capitalism, socialism, communism, about profit as a motive for economic activity, about international exploitation? What do missionaries say about the meaning of Christian love in economic relationships? Those who go as missionaries from North America to the countries of the so-called Third World need to be aware that they will be perceived as members of an exploiting society living among members of an exploited society. They will need to be conscious of the ways in which North American society, including its churches, does in fact participate in the exploitation of peoples.

In all of the above it should be clear that no missionary alone can or should define exactly what form the Christian peace witness may take in a particular environmental setting. In different parts of the world the Christian message of love and peace may be expressed in quite different ways. Local Christians will have to wrestle sincerely with these issues. A major difference between most so-called mission fields and the North American setting lies simply in that in most lands those who call themselves Christians constitute only a tiny minority of the population. The governments of these countries make no pretense of being Christian and do not recognize in any way the validity of Christian norms of conduct for the administration of national affairs. This situation will be quite different from Christendom where governments, while not following Christian norms, will often at least recognize that they should be. Thus the Christian witness to government in a country like Japan will probably take very different forms than it might take in Canada or the nations of Western Europe.

At the same time, we also need to recognize that this situation may be much nearer that of Anabaptists of the sixteenth century and also much closer to the situation in North America than we care to acknowledge. The Anabaptists, although they existed within Christendom, saw themselves as a tiny Christian minority in a sea of unbelief. They did not recognize the larger society as being a Christian one at all. Thus, as churches outside the West wrestle with the issue of a faithful expression of the peace witness of the gospel of Christ, there may be a great deal which Western Mennonite churches can learn from them, both about the expression of peace and about their own relationship to the larger society in which they live.

As we ponder the question of our missionary task in the world today, we need desperately to return to the New Testament understanding that there can be no saving faith apart from Christian living. The following of Jesus Christ, in the power of His Spirit, is in fact being saved. As we attempt to share the good news of Jesus Christ with others, we will want to show both by what we say and what we are that Jesus is in no sense a new superior object of worship to replace whatever they have worshiped up to that time. Both what Christ is and who He is as a Person are vitally important as we are called to follow Him. He is not and cannot be a sacred object to be manipulated into granting us a spiritual salvation. He is our living Lord, a Person to be followed in the way we live.

We will want to make far clearer than we have in the past that there is no such thing as a faithful disciple of Jesus Christ who does not follow Him in the way of peace. If we as missionaries do not insist on this as a basic part of the good news about Jesus Christ, then we ourselves are being unfaithful and we are deliberately helping to make unfaithful disciples. God forbid that such should ever be our role.

NOTES

Chapter 1. The Gospel of Peace

1. Reprinted with permission from *Mission-Focus*, Vol. VI, No. 1 (September 1977)

2. John Driver, *Community and Commitment* (Scottdale, Pa.: Herald Press, 1976), p. 71.

Chapter 3. Shalom Is the Mission

1. For excellent materials and biblical studies on shalom see the Shalom Curriculum of the Joint Educational Development published by the United Church Press, Philadelphia. These six major denominations chose the biblical theme of shalom as the focus for a special educational thrust in their congregations in 1973 because:

> Many people had been seeking ways to understand biblical faith from a total perspective. Shalom understood as a vision of God's ultimate intention for the world, seemed an ideal concept from which to start. ... Shalom is a broadly encompassing word to convey the heartbeat of the Bible and its vision of community, peace, and justice.—Edward A. Powers, *Signs of Shalom* (Philadelphia: United Church Press), p. 10.

It amazes me that this major thrust for peace education has so totally by-passed the Mennonites—both in terms of input and impact. This Shalom Curriculum resulted from a search for biblical foundations after consciences were awakened to war, racism, and poverty during the sixties. Mennonites could profit much by this witness to broaden their concern for nonresistance.

2. Walter Brueggemann, *Living Toward a Vision: Biblical Reflec-*

tions on Shalom (Philadelphia: United Church Press, 1976), p. 156.

3. See the dissertation by Walter Eisenbeis, *A Study of the Root Sh-L-M in the Old Testament* (Chicago: University of Chicago, 1966).

4. While the New Testament uses the Greek term *eirene* rather than *shalom*, there is growing agreement among scholars that the New Testament uses *eirene* in the sense of the Hebrew's *shalom* rather than the usage and meanings of the Greeks. We today have been greatly influenced by the Greek and Roman concepts and have largely lost the Hebraic understanding. For further documentation see my thesis, *Shalom and Mission*, at the Associated Mennonite Biblical Seminaries (1977).

5. John H. Yoder, *As You Go* (Scottdale, Pa.: Herald Press, 1961).

6. An excellent essay with this thrust is Hans-Werner Bartsch's "The Foundation and Meaning of Christian Pacifism," *New Theology No. 6*, Marty and Peerman (London: Macmillan, 1'69), p. 186-198.

Chapter 4. A Call for Evangelical Nonviolence

1. Reprinted with permission from *The Christian Century*, September 15, 1976.

2. See further my *Rich Christians in an Age of Hunger: A Biblical Study* (Downers Grove: InterVarsity Press, 1977).

3. Jacques Ellul, *Violence* (New York: Seabury Press, 1969), p. 97.

4. James Douglass, *The Non-violent Cross* (New York: Macmillan, 1968) p. 285.

5. Dale W. Brown, *Brethren and Pacifism* (Elgin, Ill.: Brethren Press, 1970), p. 121.

6. John H. Yoder, *The Politics of Jesus* (Grand Rapids: Eerdmans, 1972), p. 134.

7. Charles E. Raven, "The Renunciation of War," in Rufus M. Jones (ed.), *The Church, and the Gospel, and War* (New York: Harper and Brothers 1948), p. 5.

8. Leon Morris, "The Cross, the Center," *Christianity Today*, March 28, 1975, pp. 41-42.

9. Douglass, *op. cit.*, pp. 23-24.

10. See my *Evangelism, Salvation, and Social Justice* (Bramcote Nofts, England: Grove Books, 1977, avaiable from J. B. Houg, 1 Mechanic St., Marblehead, Maine).

11. Ellul, *op. cit.*, p. 155.

12. For an excellent manual on nonviolent direct action see Richard Taylor, *Blockade* (New York: Orbis, 1977).

Chapter 5. The Contemporary Evangelical Revival and the Peace Churches

1. The first section in this text was presented as a lecture to the Keystone Bible Institute, Lancaster, Pennsylvania, November 19, 1977.

2. Focal Pamphlet, *The Ecumenical Movement and the Faithful Church* (Scottdale, Pa.: Herald Press, 1958)

3. The remainder of the text is based upon a lecture presented to a gathering of peace church representatives attending the annual convention of the National Association of Evangelicals at Denver, Colorado, April 19, 1966. This will explain the dated quality of the quotations which it includes. It will indicate that the concern for this subject matter is not as new, as "contemporary" in the short-range sense, as might have been assumed from the assignment at Lancaster.

4. Congress of the Church's Worldwide Mission, April 9-16, 1966. Proceedings reported in the Harold Lindsell, ed., *The Church's Worldwide Mission* (Waco: Word Books, 1966).

5. Letter of September 5, 1524, addressed to Thomas Müntzer, by a group of concerned Christians at Zurich from whom Conrad Grebel did the writing, reproduced in: J. C. Wenger, ed., *Conrad Grebel's Programmatic Letters of 1524* (Scottdale, Pa.: Herald Press, 1970), pp. 29 and 39 f.

6. Alfred Larson in Lindsell, *op. cit.*, 205 f. (abridged).

7. Unfortunately it is no longer possible to find the text (a constituency relations publication of some Latin American faith mission) from which this was translated at the time.

Chapter 6. Church Growth Principles and Christian Discipleship

1. Gerald Studer, in material presented to Church Growth Seminars in the Lancaster and Franconia Mennonite conferences, fall, 1976, lists thirty places in Acts containing a direct reference to numerical growth.

2. Menno Simons, "Meditation on the Twenty-fifth Psalm," in J. C. Wenger, ed., *The Complete Writings of Menno Simons* (Scottdale, Pa.: Herald Press, 1956), p. 71

3. Donald A. McGavran, *Understanding Church growth* (Grand Rapids: Eerdmans), p. 198.

4. *Ibid.*, p. 85.

Chapter 7. Mennonite Missions and the Christian Peace Witness

1. Theron F. Schlabach, *A New Rhythm for Mennonites* (Elkhart: Mennonite Board of Missions, 1975), p. 36.

2. *Ibid.*, p. 37.

3. A. E. Janzen, "Nonresistance and Missions," in Report of the MCC Peace Section Study Conference, November 9-12, 1950, Winona Lake, Indiana, p. 128.

4. Schlabach, *op. cit.*, p. 10.

5. Walter Klaassen, *Anabaptism: Neither Catholic nor Protestant* (Waterloo, Ontario: Conrad Press, 1973). p. 20.

6. *Ibid.*, p. 47.

7. *Ibid.*, p. 56.

8. Melvin Gingerich, "The Need for a Peace Witness in the Orient," paper presented to the conjoint Council of Mission Board Secretaries/Mennonite Central Committee meeting May 1, 1959. p. 2.

9. Samuel Escobar and John Driver, *Christian Mission and Social Justice* (Scottdale, Pa.: Herald Press, 1978).

10. "A Declaration of Christian Faith and Commitment," Report of the MCC Peace Section Study Conference, November 9-12, 1950, Winona Lake, Indiana.

CONTRIBUTORS

Robert L. Ramseyer has served with the Commission
on Overseas Mission of the General Conference Mennonite Church as a missionary to Japan since 1954, and as
director of the Overseas Mission Training Center at the
Associated Mennonite Biblical Seminaries, Elkhart, Indiana, since 1970. He received the PhD degree in anthro-
pology from the University of Michigan in 1969. He and
his wife, Alice, are currently engaged in a church planting ministry in Hiroshima, Japan, where they live with
their youngest daughter, Jeanne.

Marlin E. Miller served with the Mennonite Board of
Missions in Paris, France, from 1968 to 1974, where he
began a ministry among African students in Paris and
functioned as consultant for mission board programs in
West Africa. He also represented the Mennonite Central
Committee Peace Section in Europe from 1963 to 1974.
He received the ThD degree from the University of
Heidelberg in 1968. Since 1975 he has been president
and associate professor of theology of Goshen Biblical
Seminary. He resides in Goshen, Indiana, with his wife,

Ruthann, and three children. He is a member of The Assembly, a congregation of the Mennonite Church and the General Conference Mennonite Church.

Sjouke Voolstra is pastor of three Doopsgezinde (Mennonite) congregations in the Netherlands. He has studied theology at the University of Amsterdam and at the Doopsgezinde Seminary. He is a member of the Doopsgezinde Vredesgroep (Mennonite Peace Fellowship) and contributing editor to its monthly publication. In 1977 he was a representative of the Dutch Mennonites to the Conference on Church and Peace in Bendorf, Germany.

James E. Metzler served with the Eastern Mennonite Board of Missions and Charities in Vietnam (1962-70) and in the Philippines (1971-76), witnessing through student services, relief, leadership training, and economic development. At present he is executive director of Laurelville Mennonite Church Center, Mt. Pleasant, Pennsylvania, where he resides with his wife, Rachel, and their children, Brian and Karen.

Ronald J. Sider, a member of the Brethren in Christ Church, lives with his wife, Arbutus, and three children in the Jubilee Fellowship of Germantown, a house church in an interracial section of Philadelphia. He received the PhD degree in history from Yale University in 1969. After teaching for ten years at the Temple University Campus of Messiah College he became associate professor of theology at Eastern Baptist Theological Seminary in 1977. President of Evangelicals for Social Action, he is convener of the Unit on Ethics

and Society of the Theological Commission of the World
Evangelical Fellowship, and has organized Discipleship
Workshops: Focus on Justice.

John H. Yoder served in overseas mission administration with the Mennonite Board of Missions and was
regularly involved in the meetings of the Evangelical
Foreign Mission Association and the National Association of Evangelicals. He attended the World Evangelization Conference in Lausanne in 1974. Until its mandate
expired in 1971, he was a member of the Inter-Church
Relations Committee of the Mennonite Church; he has
also served as a member of the Mennonite Central Committee Peace Section. He currently teaches theology at
Associated Mennonite Biblical Seminaries and the
University of Notre Dame.

Richard Showalter is currently serving in Hong Kong
under the Eastern Mennonite Board of Missions. He has
been a member of the faculty of Rosedale Bible Institute,
Irwin, Ohio, and served with the Mennonite Board of
Congregational Ministries in evangelism and church
growth. He is a graduate of Goshen Biblical Seminary
and has studied at the School of World Mission, Fuller
Theological Seminary. He completed a term of Voluntary Service at Downey, California, under Mennonite
Board of Missions. From 1970 to 1973 he was on the
faculty of Eastern Mennonite College. Richard and his
wife, Jewel, are the parents of three children.

MISSIONARY STUDY SERIES

Published by Herald Press, Scottdale, Pennsylvania, in association with the Institute of Mennonite Studies, Elkhart, Indiana.

1. *The Challenge of Church Growth.* A symposium edited by Wilbert R. Shenk with contributions also from John H. Yoder, Allan H. Howe, Robert L. Ramseyer, and J. Stanley Friesen (1973).

2. *Modern Messianic Movements. As a Theological and Missionary Challenge* by Gottfried Oosterwal (1973).

3. *From Kuku Hill: Among Indigenous Churches in West Africa* by Edwin and Irene Weaver (1975).

4. *Bibliography of Henry Venn's Printed Writings with Index* by Wilbert R. Shenk (1975).

5. *Christian Mission and Social Justice* by Samuel Escobar and John Driver (1978).

6. *A Spirituality of the Road* by David J. Bosch (1979).

7. *Mission and the Peace Witness: The Gospel and Christian Discipleship.* A symposium edited by Robert L. Ramseyer with contributions also from James E. Metzler, Marlin E. Miller, Richard Showalter, Ronald J. Sider, Sjouke Voolstra, and John H. Yoder (1979).

The Missionary Study Series grows out of the Mennonite Missionary Study Fellowship (MMSF) program. The MMSF is an informal fellowship of persons interested in Christian mission, meeting annually for a three-day conference on issues central to their task. It includes missionaries, mission board administrators, theologians, sociologists, and others. It is sponsored by the Institute of Mennonite Studies, 3003 Benham Avenue, Elkhart, Ind. 46514. Books in the series may be ordered from Provident Bookstores, 616 Walnut Avenue, Scottdale, Pa. 15683.

GOLDEN GATE SEMINARY LIBRARY